Lessons from Oz

Lessons from Oz

JULIENNE LA FLEUR

THE FLOWER TREE PRESS

The Flower Tree Press, Inc.
827 Hollywood Way, #179
Burbank, CA 91505

Printed in the United States of America

10 9 8 7 6 5 4 3 2

ISBN-13: 978-0-9776882-0-3

Library of Congress Control Number: 2008901624

Cover and book design by Mauna Eichner

Library of Congress Cataloging-in-Publication Data is available.

This book is printed on acid-free paper.

Contents

Preface

Lessons on how to live life come from many different places. Some people use the stories in the Bible. Some people learn what they need to know from their parents. Lately, I've been using the story about a wizard and a girl from Kansas.

I've always loved *The Wizard of Oz*. I have an Auntie Em. (Really, I do.) Ever since I was little I've identified with Dorothy. She was my idol. She had a dog, and she got to go over the rainbow. A good witch watched out for her, and she met all kinds of nice friends. She skipped and danced and sang—and she had the coolest shoes ever. (Who didn't want a pair of those shoes?)

When I watch *The Wizard of Oz*, I'm still filled with a sense of wonder. It's not just a nice story; it speaks to my spirit. It inspires, it warms, it touches my heart and makes me want to go skipping.

I realized that Dorothy is not just a typical teenager. She has principles, and she sticks to them. She is generous and loving to everyone she meets. She has innocence and confidence. She sees the truth in all things. She lives her life fully in each moment. She knows how to have fun. She is honest and strives to be the best person she can be. She makes mistakes. She is sometimes scared about what the future has in store. She loses her way. She is human. She takes her experiences and learns from them.

Dorothy's journey through Oz is an allegory that directly parallels our lives. In each scene, from the beginning of the movie to the end, a lesson can be found in Dorothy's experiences.

These lessons are good reminders of things we already know but sometimes forget—ways to be and live that make us feel great about ourselves and our lives. If we learn from these lessons, we will begin to see that our actions and positive attitudes influence the world around us, making it a better place.

Dorothy's lessons can be our lessons.

When at the end of a grumpy day, when wandering aimlessly, when meeting new friends, when battling the wicked witches in our lives, we need to remind ourselves that all of this is our Yellow Brick Road. It's our own magical journey, just like Dorothy's. In our lives, lessons from Oz are everywhere.

Lessons from Oz

Auntie Em's Advice

THE STORY

Once upon a gray Kansas day, Dorothy's dog, Toto, has chased the cat of her persnickety, crotchety, angry old hag of a neighbor, Mrs. Gulch. Mrs. G. informs Dorothy that she is calling the sheriff to take care of the wild and very dangerous terrier.

Dorothy comes home nervous, upset and fearful of what might happen to Toto. She tries explaining her predicament to Uncle Henry and Auntie Em, but they are busy counting their chickens after they've hatched. She tries to get advice from the farmhands. While walking across the fence to the hog pen, she ends up falling in and is almost trampled by a dozen or so big muddy hogs until she is rescued.

Auntie Em comes by to scold the farmhands and tells them to get back to work. Dorothy again tries to talk to her.

> **Dorothy**
>
> Auntie Em, really—you know what Miss Gulch said she was gonna do to Toto? She said she was gonna—
>
> **Auntie Em**
>
> Now, Dorothy, dear, stop imagining things. You always get yourself into a fret over nothing. Now, you just help us out today, and find yourself a place where you won't get into any trouble.

THE LESSON

We think Auntie Em is just trying to get Dorothy out of her hair for a while, but her advice is actually quite good.

"Stop imagining things. You always get yourself into a fret over nothing."

Ninety-five percent of fretting is over nothing. That is the nature of fretting—worrying needlessly.

Dorothy is fearful because Mrs. Gulch has threatened to take Toto. If we pause the movie at this moment, it does appear that Dorothy is working herself into quite a frenzy. She is probably thinking something like, "What's going to happen to Toto? That crazy woman is going to take him away. I love my dog. She can't do that. I need to stop her. What am I going to do? I need help." So when she tells Auntie Em and Uncle Henry and they don't respond, she feels even more helpless and desperate. Her thoughts start racing: "Toto is going to die! I need to save him. I don't want to live without him!"

When we have what looks like a potential problem in our lives, we usually do what Dorothy does. We start imagining the worst possible outcome or dozens of equally horrible scenarios.

Let's take a work problem. We go to lunch, and when we come back, our boss has left us a curt message. She sounds a little stern and says, "Please come to my office as soon as you can."

"Uh-oh," we think. "I'm in trouble."

Then we go over all the questionable things we have done in the past week that the boss could be calling about. The worst-case scenario may even cross our mind—that we're going to be fired.

We start envisioning how the meeting with our boss will go. What are we going to say to defend ourselves? What are we going to do? Where will we look for another job?

We're in a panic, and we have not even talked to our boss. We need to stop, take a moment to calm down and look at the facts. What has happened, really? Our boss has called and left a message and needs to see us. In most situations, if we stick to the facts, the fretting can be immediately dismissed.

All that other stuff is our minds working overtime. Our imaginings are so powerful, they actually transport us to that circumstance, and we feel all the emotions of a dilemma that doesn't even exist. Usually we don't stop at one painful scene; we are very creative and concoct at least two or three. We feel all the emotions of all three scenarios, and it's no wonder we are upset.

Dorothy is imagining her life without her dog; of course she's upset. She would have gone on worrying about it for the next few hours if Auntie Em hadn't told her to stop it.

Worrying is useless because we cannot predict the future. At this point in the movie, Mrs. Gulch could change her mind or get hit by a tractor on the way over to the sheriff's. Dorothy cannot know what will happen. Sure, we can fast-forward the movie and see that the dog gets taken away, but all that time leading up to it did not have to be spent in a panic.

We all know worrying is a waste of time and energy. It's not going to make the outcome any better, but we do it anyway. We are really good at it. We could win contests.

It's as if one person has given us all the same bad advice: "When I start feeling a little anxious, let me tell you what tends to help me. The moment I wake up in the morning, I start to worry. I'm not talking a little bit of worrying. I'm talking serious worrying. The kind of worrying that is so negative that every scenario ends up in some sort of life-altering personal disaster. What a rush! I worry until I get a stomachache and can't get to sleep. What's so amazing about that is, then, I have the entire night to worry some more. All night! Consumed with worry! I love it. It's so helpful! I highly recommend it."

We know that's crazy, but we do all those things.

Whether or not Mrs. Gulch comes to take the dog is not the issue; it's how Dorothy spends the time in between.

Take Auntie Em's advice. Don't get yourself into a fret over nothing. Stay calm, and wait to see if it's really something.

Sing About It

Dorothy is wandering around the farm and pondering the idea of a place without trouble. She has a vision of exactly what that would look like for her. Her dream place. She sings:

> Somewhere, over the rainbow, way up high,
> There's a land that I heard of once in a lullaby.
> Somewhere, over the rainbow, skies are blue.
> And the dreams that you dare to dream really do come true.
> Someday I'll wish upon a star,
> And wake up where the clouds are far behind me.
> Where troubles melt like lemon drops,
> Away above the chimney tops, that's where you'll find me.
> Somewhere, over the rainbow, bluebirds fly.
> Birds fly over the rainbow, why then—oh, why can't I?
> If happy little bluebirds fly beyond the rainbow,
> Why, oh, why, can't I?

THE LESSON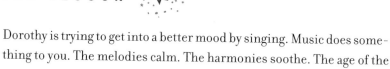

Dorothy is trying to get into a better mood by singing. Music does some-thing to you. The melodies calm. The harmonies soothe. The age of the musical has been gone long enough. We need to sing more!

Pick a song, any song that gets you in a better mood immediately. Keep a copy with you at all times. When you're in your car, and you're having a bad day, roll up the windows and sing at the top of your lungs. Who cares if the person in the car next to you thinks you look silly. At work, lock your office door, put on your headphones, and jam.

If you feel creative, try singing your very own made-up ditty. If you aren't that musically inclined, it's easy to take the ever-popular "Row, Row, Row Your Boat" tune and see if you can come up with your own fun lyrics to bemoan your troubles: "Oh, no, no, my beau/just broke up with me,/but he's a selfish son of a blank,/and I'll kick him in the . . . knee." Or something like: "Oh, no, no, my boss/is being such a jerk,/but I will just sing this song/until I get off work." (You'd better sing that one silently to yourself!) Or perhaps a generic version: "Oh, no, no, my life/is going straight to hell,/but I am just going to sing,/and it will turn out well." You get the idea, so pick a rhyme and sing about your quandary.

Yes, it's the corniest thing you could do in any situation, but it'll make you laugh instead of getting more and more upset. It takes what you think is a serious problem and makes it sound a bit better so that your thoughts aren't stuck in a constant loop of negative fixation.

Next time you're in a mood, stop for a moment and think, "If I were Dorothy, what would I be singing right now?" State your problem in ten words or less, and you have the title of your song.

Try to picture your life as a musical. What would you be doing? Would it be melodramatic? Would you be lying down swooning over a lost love? Would you be mopey? What would you be wearing? Would there be any Pips to accompany you?

Break into song like Dorothy—it just might cheer you up.

Somewhere Over Your Rainbow

THE STORY

Somewhere over Dorothy's rainbow, "way up high/There's a land that I heard of once in a lullaby/ . . . troubles melt like lemon drops/Away above the chimney tops . . . /If happy little bluebirds fly . . . /Why, oh, why, can't I?"

THE LESSON

At first glance, the words to the song seem naive and no more meaningful than a child's nursery rhyme. But Dorothy is painting a picture of what her perfect life would look like on the other side of the rainbow.

We all do that. We spend a lot of time dreaming about that perfect place somewhere over our rainbows. The one thing Dorothy, you and I agree on is it would be great if our dreams could become a reality. The problem is that sometimes we don't know exactly how we think and feel about our dreams.

So I've come up with a simple exercise to help you figure that out. Clear your mind for ten seconds. I'm serious—start counting and clearing. (One one thousand, two one thousand . . .)

Oh, come on.

Just try it.

Clear your mind, and count to ten.

Now turn the page.

The dreams that you dare to dream
really do come true.

Just now, what did you think about that phrase—the first thought that popped into your head? Write it down.

Was it positive or negative? Was it indifferent? Were you amused, or were you mad? Do you think it's true? Do you think it's a load of crap? What do you like about that phrase? What don't you like?

That, whatever you thought, is how you feel about your dreams. If you thought, "Not for me they don't," you feel that your dreams don't come true. If you thought, "That's a bunch of hooey," then you feel that your dreams are a bunch of hooey. (What is hooey, anyway?) If you thought, "Oh, that's nice," then you feel that your dreams are just nice thoughts.

Dorothy thinks dreams only come true in that magical fairyland over the rainbow. If we think like Dorothy, then our dreams won't ever materialize.

Maybe we should first talk about the kinds of dreams we have.

We have all had ideas like Dorothy's. We wish that we could fly like a bluebird, that our troubles would melt like lemon drops, that a money tree would grow in our backyard. Or, perhaps, that if we ate any sort of chocolate, we would instantly shed five pounds. Over my rainbow I would have all the powers of Samantha on *Bewitched*. I would wiggle my nose so that cleaning, cooking and laundry would never be a problem. These are not dreams; these are fantasies, things that are entirely impossible in our given reality.

The difference between a fantasy and a dream is that a dream can come true. I will never be able to wiggle my nose and get rid of soap scum, but I can hire someone to clean my house. I'll never have wings to fly, but I can learn to fly a plane or hang glide. I will never have a money tree, but I can make a lot of money.

By taking a look at the subtle difference between dreams and fantasies, you can start to change your thinking about your dreams. Make sure they are based in reality.

In addition to knowing how we feel about our dreams, the next step toward getting our dreams is making sure we know they can and will come true for us. We've all had dreams, and we've all had dreams come true. Where do we get all these other ideas—that dreams are not possible, that they're silly, that dreams-come-true happen only to other people?

At some point we learned to stop dreaming, to be more practical, to "not get our hopes up." That is one of the silliest phrases taught by parents everywhere. Why not get your hopes up? Trying to stop your hope is like telling a child not to get excited about Christmas. Hope, according to the dictionary, is "a feeling that what is wanted will happen." If we could stop that feeling, we would never get excited about our lives, and we would never strive for anything better.

Sometimes we try not to hope so we may avoid disappointment, hurt and failure. When we try to avoid experiencing emotions we don't like, we are limited to doing only those things that seem comfortable and easy. And let's face it, our dreams are big! Gigantic! Awesome! You don't accomplish anything big, gigantic or awesome by sitting on your sofa watching TV and eating Cheetos. We might have to work very hard, risk something, feel uncomfortable, maybe even be scared or upset. All these feelings usually happen when we try to change a very big aspect of our lives, like starting a new relationship or getting a new job.

Another disheartening phrase we've all heard is, "Stop dreaming and face reality." Whose reality are we facing? If you take a look, there are a gazillion amazing stories from incredible people about how they made their dreams a reality. Those amazing stories are out there in books, magazines, newspapers, on TV—real stories from real people who have made their dreams come true.

Ask your friends and family to tell you examples of dreams that came true for them. Ask people you meet in line at the grocery store. It happens to everyone, all the time. Sometimes we forget that.

Think of an example in your life when you had a dream and it came true. When we were little, we all got that toy we begged for. In high school we all dreamed of the day we could drive. We have all dreamed of getting a new job or a better place to live. How many of your dreams have you had come true? Start a list. I bet that in your life you've had at least twenty dreams come true—maybe even fifty. Imagine that—you are a dream-come-true machine.

Once we've established that dreams can and do come true, it's easier for us to accept that possibility for our lives. We will know that "the dreams that we dare to dream really do come true," and we'll start dreaming bigger dreams.

What about you? What's your dream?

Dare to dream.

Come on, I dare you.

Better yet, I double-dare you to make it come true.

Cry on Your Bed

THE STORY

After the singing of "Over the Rainbow," Mrs. Gulch arrives at Dorothy's house armed with a letter from the sheriff permitting her to take Toto away to be put to sleep. Uncle Henry and Auntie Em wimp out and let Mrs. Gulch take the dog. Dorothy runs into her room in tears.

THE LESSON

If all else fails—you've tried to turn your day around by singing, and by thinking a little more positively, and it just gets worse and worse—cry on your bed! An anguished wail to the heavens makes you feel better.

We need to take time to cry and let it all out. We need to acknowledge, "Hey, I'm really hurting here!" Frustration, anger, disappointment, sadness and all those bottled-up emotions are released. Sometimes we suppress all that stuff. We try to have a stiff upper lip, try not to be a baby, or try not to let whatever it is "get to us" for whatever reason. We forget that we need to let go of those emotions.

Remember when you were a little kid and you would plop down on the floor and kick and scream until you had gotten all those feelings out? Try it sometime. (Preferably when no one is around.) It's actually quite an immediate stress reliever.

We've all cried ourselves to sleep. The morning after the big cry always seems so much better. Why is that? The facts and circumstances surrounding whatever we were crying about do not change one bit overnight.

Crying gives us a fresh perspective. It allows the emotional part of us to get out of the way and clears a path for more rational thinking. Often we get new insights and see new ways to solve our problem. We always feel better after a good cry—sometimes we even think better. (Maybe all of the above reasons are why we call it a "good" cry.)

Dorothy knew that when all else fails, and you've given up, the best thing to do is just fling yourself onto your pillow and let the waterworks begin.

Note: A good ending to a good cry is eating some Ben & Jerry's (not found in Oz) and watching reruns of *I Love Lucy*. (It always works for me.)

Running Away

 **THE STORY**

Mrs. Gulch pedals her bicycle down a dusty road with Toto riding in a basket. (Dunt da-dunt da-da dum. Dunt da-dunt da-da dum.) Toto jumps out and runs home to Dorothy. He leaps through her bedroom window and greets Dorothy with a face licking.

Dorothy is overjoyed. However, she still needs to solve the problem of Mrs. Gulch's wanting to kill Toto. The only option available, as she sees it, is to run away. So they do. Armed with a small suitcase and a basket, Dorothy and Toto start down another dirt road into the wilds of Kansas.

THE LESSON

We have all heard that "you shouldn't run away from your problems." Why not?

Eventually we'll have to face our problems; they follow us wherever we go. We can put a lot of distance between ourselves and our problems, but they will catch up to us. Often we don't put actual physical distance between ourselves and our problems; sometimes it's just a mental distance called "avoidance."

Running away or avoiding problems falls under the category of denial. *The Oxford American Dictionary* defines the word *problem* as "something that has to be accomplished or dealt with." If we run away or do not deal with our problem, it doesn't just vanish because it's in another state or because we've decided not to think about it.

Dorothy runs away because her neighbor wants to kill her dog. Does running away solve that problem? Not really. It gets Toto away from the situation, that's true, but Mrs. Gulch still wants to kill him.

There's a scene that's missing from the movie. It's Mrs. Gulch arriving at the sheriff's in a pool of sweat after pedaling all that way. She opens the basket and Toto is missing. She is fuming. In fact, if she sees that damn dog again, she'll probably be so damn mad she'll kill it her damn self. So Dorothy not only hasn't solved her problem by putting distance between Toto and Mrs. Gulch; she actually may have made it bigger.

In addition to perhaps aggravating the problem, Dorothy has created some new ones: She has no home, no money, no food, no idea where she is going, and she ends up getting caught in the midst of a tornado.

Running away from problems rather than staying and trying to work through them can create much bigger problems than we ever anticipate. Dorothy found that out the hard way. Instead of running away, run right into them—solve them and be done with them.

When Life Gets Stormy

THE STORY

The gray Kansas day starts to get grayer as a storm approaches. Dorothy and Toto stumble upon a curious soothsayer named Professor Marvel. He reads Dorothy's fortune and persuades her to go back home. With a tornado looming, they rush back to the farm, only to find it abandoned, with Auntie Em and Uncle Henry safely locked in the storm cellar without them. The eye of the cyclone is upon them, so Dorothy and Toto seek shelter in the house. A heavy gust of wind blows a window frame right into Dorothy's head, and she's knocked unconscious.

THE LESSON

Let's just review Dorothy's day, shall we?

Mrs. Gulch threatens to take her dog. Dorothy comes home, and nobody cares. She falls into a hog patch. Her aunt scolds her. Her dog is taken away to be killed; luckily, he escapes. Dorothy runs away from home. She runs back home. She is caught in a tornado. Her family abandons her. A window hits her in the head. She is knocked unconscious.

We've all had days where, at about 2:00 p.m., we'd like to go home, crawl into bed and say, "I'll just try this again tomorrow." Too bad that's usually not an option.

Those days really are like the weather. We wake up, and it's sunny, and we think it's going to be a nice day. One little thing happens—a light shower. We deal with it, and then another and another! Ugh! Soon our day becomes a torrential downpour.

Sometimes our storms get worse the more we try do deal with them. In the middle of one of those days, we get mad: "This day isn't going as planned! This should not be happening to me!"

These two statements, which we've all uttered, are what make it worse. In addition to trying to fix our problems, we're getting mad about them. The idea that this should not be happening to us starts to get us more upset. It *is* happening to us—in fact, there is no other way for our lives to happen.

Sometimes we take our bad days personally. We think, "What did I do?" "Am I being punished?" Stop yourself from taking it personally. We could all pull out our long list of faults and start to think of all the reasons why we are, in fact, horrible people and somehow deserve this day, but why go there?

My minister, Marlene Morris, once explained how problems in our lives are sometimes just as arbitrary as the weather. She talked about how we get mad at the rain, and how silly that is because we know it has to rain or everything will die, but sometimes we curse it anyway. The rain didn't know we were planning a picnic. It's just taking care of business, and that can interfere with our plans, so we have to adjust (or use an umbrella and try not to care when we get a little wet).

When the big problems are pelting us full force, we start to think, "What could I have done differently?" "What did I do wrong?" "If I could turn back the clock, I wouldn't have . . ." This just starts us on the path to beating ourselves up. Objectively look at your hand in this mess another day, not while it's happening.

Sometimes we blame someone or something else. "If only he hadn't done such-and-such, then this wouldn't have happened." Sometimes we make it worse by calling that person up in the heat of anger and telling them that our bad day is their fault. First we had a problem, and then we created a conflict with another person out of it. It just gets messier from there.

We need to accept that this day is happening and decide we are going to deal with it. That's what Dorothy did. She returned home in the middle of a terrible storm to try to deal with her day. Unfortunately, it was so out of control at that point that all she could do was to run into the house and try to stay safe.

When we're in the midst of one of life's storms, we just have to know that it will blow over. We need to seek shelter, take cover and know that storms don't last forever. The sun will come out tomorrow. Oops, sorry, wrong musical.

Munchkinland

 **T H E   S T O R Y**

Dorothy wakes up to find that her house is being carried up, up, up and away in a funnel cloud of doom until it lands with a thump. She opens the front door and tentatively walks, with Toto in her arms, into a magical new land, the splendor of colors that is Munchkinland.

She wanders around in awe of the deserted yet beautiful place over the rainbow, eyes as big as saucers, and her mouth agape at the wonder of all she sees.

Dorothy
Toto—I've a feeling we're not in Kansas anymore.

Be a Good Witch

 **THE STORY**

A giant pink bubble floats down from the sky. Glinda the Good Witch of the North appears. She is fluffy and pink. Cotton candy to the eyes. She speaks to Dorothy.

Glinda
Are you a good witch or a bad witch?

Dorothy
Who, me? Why, I'm not a witch at all.
I'm Dorothy Gale from Kansas.

Glinda
Oh.

Glinda tells Dorothy the Munchkins are under the impression she is a witch because her house landed on the Witch of the East (killing her instantly). Dorothy explains it was an accident, but either way, the Munchkins are delighted. They thank her. They sing. They dance. There is much hoopla in her honor. Apparently that woman from the East was not so very nice to the Munchkins.

THE LESSON

In the land over the rainbow, witches are clearly defined. Good witches are beautiful and live in the North. Bad witches are hideously ugly and live in the East and West. Wouldn't it be great if people were marked as clearly? All good people would float around in bubbles and wear pink; all bad people would have green skin and ride on broomsticks. Much, much simpler.

We associate most witches with evil, but we can be whatever sort of witches we like.

Everything Glinda does is good. Behind her every spell is the intention of creating more and more magical, good things. We can treat our lives as if we are good witches. The two most important rules for being a good witch are to be good and to do good. (Yes, I know, it seems pretty obvious.)

Remember when your mom told you to "be good"? She wanted you to be polite and nice and to behave. We can take it one step further if we are to live up to our goodness potential. Behind every thought, every action, every word, should be good.

We can be aware of what we are doing and how it will affect others. We should always ask ourselves, "Is this good? Who will this help? Will this harm or hurt anyone else in any way?"

We can try to "do the right thing." Practice the Golden Rule: "Do unto others as you would have others do unto you."

In addition to being good, we can strive to do as much good as we can. Glinda welcomes Dorothy, a complete stranger, to Munchkinland. When she finds out she's in trouble (yes, I'm jumping ahead in the story), she gives her the ruby slippers to keep her safe. She directs her down the Yellow Brick Road to Emerald City to find the Wizard, who can help her get back to Kansas. She checks in every once in a while to make sure Dorothy's okay. All that is above and beyond the call of duty for someone she only talked to for five minutes.

The other secret to being a good witch is to have faith in yourself and your spells. We need to recognize that everything we do will turn out with the best possible result, even if, in the middle of the magic, it doesn't look so hot. At a few points during the movie I think, "Why did Glinda give her those slippers? If she hadn't, the Witch might have left her alone." But Glinda knew what she was doing. She didn't give Dorothy the ruby slippers and say, "Here, these might keep you safe, but then again, you could be killed." She waved her magic wand and in that moment knew absolutely, positively, that everything was going to work out okay for Dorothy.

How many times do we put a plan in motion or make a decision and then get wishy-washy about it? "Will this turn out all right? Will this work? Did I do the wrong thing? Did I make a mistake?" Try to stop second-guessing yourself.

Be a good witch all the time. Do as much good as you can. Have confidence in your spells and know that whatever you are doing, it's all good.

Even Wicked Witches Have Family

THE STORY

Everything is great in Munchkinland for about three musical numbers and a whole lot of dancing. Dorothy is honored, showered with flowers, and a tiny twitching trio presents her with a gigantic lollipop.

Then the Wicked Witch of the West, sister of the dead one, shows up. She seems to be more than a little upset at the passing of her sister.

THE LESSON

The Witch is obviously a bundle of negativity (hence the "wicked" title). However, let's take a look at the situation from her point of view. She arrives in Munchkinland to find her sister crushed to death, and four hundred height-challenged people are dancing around singing about how great that is. ("Ding-dong, the Witch is dead!")

She and her sister were probably very close. After all, they grew up in the same dysfunctional family. They were probably teased as tiny witches about their green skin and pointy hats and noses. They probably shared many things—magic spells and their love of funny striped stockings. They probably felt like misfits "over the rainbow" with all those super-happy people dressed in colors. So they acted out their aggression, perhaps in negative ways.

The Witch has just found out her sister has died, and she has every right to be upset. Who wouldn't be?

The Witch is not in touch with her emotions and can't let out the hurt and loss she is feeling for her sister's sudden catastrophe. She is trying to deal with the pain of no more hemlock tea parties, no more sharing wart-enhancement secrets, no more cackling over the cauldron about that time they turned their parents into field mice and the cat ended up finding them.

Behind any big anger is a really big hurt. Anger is most often an outward reaction to something that touches us very deeply on the inside. The only way the Witch can deal with her pain is to turn it into anger. She is reacting the only way she knows how. She needs to blame someone, and the most convenient person is Dorothy.

How many times do we get angry instead of feeling hurt? How many times do we blame someone else for our hurt feelings? Try to remember the last time you were truly angry with someone. What were you angry about? Underneath was a frustration, a disappointment, a sadness—some other unexpressed emotion. We need to allow ourselves to feel the true emotions instead of masking them with anger. Of course the Wicked Witch seems wicked—anger is the only emotion she allows herself to feel. If we consistently disregard our other emotions and turn them into anger, one day we'll become as mean, bitter and horrible as the Wicked Witch of the West.

We need to look at the anger in our lives and make sure we are not repressing some deeper emotion. We need to try to understand the wicked witches of our lives and know they are not really that wicked, just emotionally green.

Who Killed My Sister?

 **THE STORY**

So the Witch is upset that her sister has kicked the bucket. She is seething and wants to know, "Who is responsible?" She slinks around looking for the possible murderess. Her bony green-bean finger points in Dorothy's direction.

Witch

Who killed my sister?

Who killed the Witch of the East?

Was it you?

Dorothy

No, no! It was an accident!

I didn't mean to kill anybody!

THE LESSON

People need to find the cause of accidents. It's understandable. Something went wrong, and either we or the people we love are hurt. Our instincts are to protect ourselves and the people closest to us. That's why, like the Witch, we want to hunt down the hurter and let them have it in a tit-for-tat way. But I'd argue that what we really want is to go back in time and erase the accident completely. Since we can't do that, making someone pay for that hurt seems like the next best thing.

And here in the Oz story, this accident, on the scale of accidents, has pretty much broken the needle. An out-of-control house (with Dorothy and Toto, too) has fallen on a person. A very mean person—but still, we are talking about a death here.

Was it Dorothy's fault? No, she had no part in the death of the Witch's sister. It was clearly an accident. But the Witch needs someone to blame. She couldn't start yelling at the house, the actual perpetrator of doom, because it's no darn fun yelling at shingles. She needed someone to yell at.

If this were a real incident, the Witch would be hiring a high-powered attorney to sue the light blue socks off of Dorothy for wrongful death for $1.7 million. Then Dorothy would sue the builders of the house, because the house did not stay bolted to the foundation, and the builders of the house would sue the bolt company. The bolt company would then sue the place they purchased the metal from, and the metal place would surely find someone to sue.

When accidents happen and people we love get hurt, it's okay to try to figure out what went wrong. It's okay to find out if someone was negligent. What's not okay is putting the blame where it might not belong, just to blame someone or something.

In a world filled with one accident after another, we seem to have forgotten that sometimes people get hurt for no reason at all. Sometimes terrible things happen and no one is responsible—it's a hard pill to swallow. The onslaught of court cases has made us believe that someone is always to blame. Our litigious society always seems to attach a monetary value to an accident, from the tiniest mishap to the biggest catastrophe.

Before blaming someone, first ask, "Did this person mean to hurt someone? Does the person show remorse? Is any one person to blame, or was it just a cataclysmic event that was unforeseeable or unavoidable?"

Accidents happen in the world—some tiny spills and some big, heartbreaking ones, and sometimes, even though it hurts, no one is to blame.

I'd Kill for Those Shoes

 **THE STORY**

The Witch, still fuming at Dorothy, suddenly remembers her sister's prized possession. Sticking out from beneath Dorothy's fallen house are two witch legs, adorned in the classic black-and-white-striped stocking, set off very nicely by the most beautiful pair of glittering red shoes. But before the Wicked Witch has a chance to get them, Glinda instantly transports these very powerful magic shoes onto Dorothy's feet in order to keep her safe.

THE LESSON

They sparkle, they radiate, and they shine. They are the coolest shoes you've ever seen. I can't imagine a little girl who did not want a pair of ruby slippers after seeing this movie. Hell, I still have shoe envy big time, but now that I'm a grown-up, I don't know where I'd wear them. They seem so impractical; yet whenever someone mentions them, I get a pang mixed with a twinge of excitement and that old familiar longing for a pair of ruby slippers.

What is it about those ruby slippers? They are quite beautiful, it's true. Jeweled shoes are very hard to come by, even now. If you found an actual pair of slippers Judy Garland wore in the movie in the back of your closet and had a garage sale, you could buy yourself a spectacular new house—the last time a pair sold at auction, they went for over six hundred and fifty thousand dollars. If you could get your hands on the pair made by Harry Winston with forty-six hundred real rubies and more than fifty carats of diamond trim, you could retire right now with at least a cool three million.

Their material worth was not what intrigued me as a six-year-old. It was that they were magical (and, of course, the shimmering was an added cool effect). But even if they were green-turd moccasins, I would have wanted a pair because of their intrinsic powers. Powers that went beyond the ordinary. They could keep you safe from a crazed green hag, and if you knew how to use them correctly, they could transport you wherever you wanted to go. And they seemed to have other, untold enchanting powers.

I remember using these powers on a daily basis. Back then, magic shoes would have enhanced my arsenal greatly. I already had a magic wand, a flying carpet and a genie named Mr. Peanut Butter and Jelly Sandwich. A six-year-old can't ever have too many supernatural abilities. Besides, the ruby slippers would have gone nicely with my gown and tiara—my glass slippers were getting kind of tired.

I am sad to say that I have used none of those powers lately, nor have I attended any balls, or kissed any frogs that turned into princes. As I gaze into my closet filled with clothes, there's not a single magic cloak. I have not limped around the house, one shoe on, one shoe off, muttering, "Jeez, what happened to my other magic plum Prada?" It seems I have lost my belief in magic—hence my pang whenever the ruby slippers are mentioned.

Like most grown-ups, I've seen one too many behind-the-magic specials. I am old and jaded and want my magic back. I don't want to know that rabbits don't come out of hats and carpets don't fly and new shoes won't keep you safe, but they might give you a fresh, painful blister.

We can never fully recapture that magic we had when we were kids, but we can try to get some of it back. We may be older, but our ability to use our imaginations to play, dress up and pretend is still stashed away in a drawer. Every once in a while, we need to take it out and run with it.

Go to a magic show and just enjoy the magic—try to lose the skeptic within that wants to figure out the tricks. "Ooh" and "aah" at the rabbit coming out of the hat, and hold your breath when the magician saws that woman in half instead of wondering exactly how she's bending like that.

Have a tea party, and by all means dress up. Instruct all your friends to make up fancy names and tell stories about themselves—but with only one rule: Nothing can be the truth! See how outrageous you can be. "The mansion is coming along, but we don't seem to have room between the north wing and the west wing to put in the northwest wing." "My date last night with Matthew McConaughey went smashingly well, but, I don't know, George Clooney keeps saying he wants a commitment, and I'm not sure I'm ready. What to do?"

Ask a girlfriend to go to the mall, and make appointments for makeovers at the cosmetics counter. Then go try on all the evening gowns you can find. Playing dress-up is fun, especially if you venture into those stores that you'd ordinarily never dare to. Go ahead, try on evening wear that costs thousands of dollars. Imagine walking down a red carpet with rose petals at your feet, or dancing in a field in the moonlight.

Beware: This next suggestion is only for the brave. Be a princess for a day. Get a tiara (the more sparkly the better), and wear it with jeans and a T-shirt all day. People are surprisingly supportive, and little girls are quite complimentary. More than once a little girl has commented that she loved my tiara. I always reply with a "What, this old thing?" and a wink. Some people may ask why you are wearing this lovely accessory, and I've found the best response is, "Because I'm a princess. Duh!" Most people will just smile and think one of two things: "What a lunatic!" or "What a sense of whimsy!" Who cares what they're thinking? You've made someone smile.

Last but not least, go shopping. (I had to include one lesson with shopping.) Buy a pair of gorgeous shoes, and as you slip them on your feet, imagine these are your very own magic shoes. They will keep you safe, and they will take you where you need to go, one magical step at a time. They have whatever powers you need them to have. No one but you knows what they do, and no one else knows that you are wearing them. It's your little secret. It's fun just to daydream with them on. Where would you go if you could go anywhere? What other sorts of magical powers do they have? As you sit at your desk listening to so-and-so go on about this and that, you can think to yourself, "I've got magic shoes on, la-ti-da-ti-da." You can look at all your coworkers and feel bad that they paid so much good money for their boring everyday shoes. During the day you can leave magic footprints—wherever you go, you glow, and when the sun goes down, there's a phosphorescent trail where you have traveled. You can smile quietly to yourself as the office is in a tizzy. Not to worry, you can click your heels and be out of there at any time.

Pretty soon you'll be able to feel the magic floating back in, as if someone has sprinkled a little fairy dust into your life, and you'll know a little secret—that there is such a thing as Santa Claus and you are not limited by this stuffy old grown-up existence. You'll remember the little girl who was once you, who had so much fun. She's still in there ready to fly and click her heels and transform her everyday self into whatever she wants to be. You can summon her—your whimsical inner you—any time you need to. As long as there are shopping malls, you can be transformed—never again will you underestimate the power of a new pair of shoes.

And Your Little Dog Too!

 **THE STORY**

Glinda has given Dorothy the ruby slippers. Dorothy is gazing at her feet, wondering what the heck happened. And the Wicked Witch is beyond mad. She wants those slippers—no matter what. Glinda tells her to scram because she's got no power in Munchkinland. The Witch is just about to leave when she utters those famous last words to Dorothy:

> **Witch**
> I'll get you, my pretty. And your little dog too!

THE LESSON

Don't threaten people. It's not nice. It's a lot more than just not nice—it ends up turning on you. Few of us are ever of Wicked Witch proportions, but we might toss a not-so-nice thought around every once in a while, maybe a muttering, an evil slip o' the tongue in a moment of anger. It happens.

Threatening people is just a knee-jerk reaction to our anger—an act of retaliation. Someone harms us, and we want to harm them back. It would be great if life were like the board game Life, and when we were wronged, we could use that Revenge square and send someone back ten spaces, but unfortunately, we are not playing a game.

Powerlessness is what we are really feeling when we threaten or try to take revenge on people. The Witch in this situation could not save her sister, so she channels the anger and hurt she is feeling into a desire to take revenge on Dorothy.

When we decide to make sure whoever hurt us gets theirs, we are sending a cosmic boomerang out into the world. Call it karma. It doesn't matter that the person hurt you first or that they deserve what you might do to them. Whether you yell at them, tell them off, hurt them back or make them miserable, all it does is make sure you get more of the same in your life later. Sure, you might get a quick fix and some personal satisfaction from knowing you retaliated, but remember what happened to the Witch at the end of the movie? That was just the logical conclusion to a life of revenge and bitterness.

Of course, we don't react as strongly as the Wicked Witch. Most of us don't go around trying to kill innocent young girls for their cool shoes. But we do utter threatening words. Sometimes we act on those threatening words. Next time you are trying to give someone a taste of their own medicine to see how they like it, stop and ask yourself, "How did this person hurt my feelings?"

Trying to uncover those feelings is hard to do. It takes time, and it also takes a willingness to try to work through them instead of just lobbing that hurt right back over the net. Can you let them know how you are feeling and deal with the conflict?

Why do you feel powerless, and what can you do to make sure this does not happen again? Try to answer those questions.

Know that you will get through it, with grace and wisdom and sense enough to know that no matter how mad you are at someone else, hurting them will not make your hurt go away. Only you can do that.

Don't be like the Wicked Witch. Threatening or taking revenge is never a good idea.

Getting Out of Oz

 **THE STORY**

The Wicked Witch of the West exits Munchkinland in a puff of red smoke. Glinda the Good Witch tells Dorothy she'd best get out of Oz because the Wicked Witch seems to be her enemy. She advises Dorothy that to get back to Kansas, she'll need the help of the Wizard of Oz.

Glinda
He lives in the Emerald City,
and that's a long journey from here.
Did you bring your broomstick with you?

Dorothy
No, I'm afraid I didn't.

Glinda
Well, then, you'll have to walk.

THE LESSON

On the long journeys of our lives, the pursuing of dreams, the chasing of rainbows, we can only walk.

When ascending Mount Everest, some climbers take a helicopter up to a certain point, but to get to the tip-top, they have to go on foot. Dorothy has no broomstick, no quick way to get from A to B, so she must hoof it.

No one walks anymore. (That's why God invented cars, isn't it?) A long journey to us is a ten-hour flight to Europe. Getting from New York City to Los Angeles takes a mere six hours. Imagine the pioneers. It would take them up to six months in horse-drawn wagons, a treacherous and often deadly trip.

Walking seems so slow. Moving forward step by step to get anywhere is an antiquated concept that was thrown out with the modern technologies of the twentieth century.

We are bombarded with the idea that we can do anything in thirty minutes or less—get a pizza, do our taxes, become millionaires if we pick the right stock at the right time. For only thirty minutes a day, we can start our own business, learn to speak French or have great abs.

We are so pummeled with this thirty-minute mentality, it's no wonder we feel as if things happen too slowly. We are frustrated when things take longer than we think they should. Our kids have less and less persistence because they are force-fed this notion of quick and easy. Our society has forgotten about teaching patience, diligence and reasonable time expectations.

The people who become rich are the ones who saved slowly, invested long term and, over the course of thirty years (not minutes), became financially independent. Successful people do not wake up one morning to find they've magically become the president of a huge corporation. It takes years of hard work. Most celebrities work on their careers for decades before they get recognition. We don't hear about the years of waiting tables, the long workouts and thousands of sit-ups. We envy their fame, fortune and six-pack abs now.

Like Dorothy's trip through Oz, our journeys will take time. Whether it's changing careers, quitting smoking or losing weight, we need to make sure that we realize how long what we set out to do will take, and sometimes the answer might be years. Sometimes we may not even know the time frame, but all we can do is start out and see where we go, with an open mind and realistic ideas about our achievements. It's great to aim high, but to aim so high that we will almost certainly feel like we are failing is self-defeating. We can get discouraged and give up. Remember the story of the tortoise and the hare—slow and steady will get you there.

As you start out on your journey, walk at a nice pace (figuratively, that is). We can't take a broomstick, or a race car, for that matter. If you did go by race car, what would you see? What would you learn? What would you be able to experience but high-powered acceleration and the roar of the engine, blurred landscapes and the smell of exhaust?

If Dorothy had taken a broomstick, what would she have seen traveling through the sky and looking down? What would she have experienced? Well, she wouldn't have met her buddies along the path, friends who helped see that she got to the Emerald City and saved her from the clutches of the Witch. She had to learn a lesson before she could get home. That is what her journey was all about.

Our journeys, while we may think they are to get from A to B, are more about the trip than the goal. We need to skip down the road, meet friends and grow as people. The experiences that make up the journey are where the learning occurs and a major part of how we get to where we are going. If we knew everything already, we wouldn't be on the journey. Each road and individual journey is different. Your path to wherever you need to go is beautiful and unique. You might traverse it for a while, so it's best to appreciate it. Enjoy the walk, and try to learn what you can from it.

On the long journeys of our lives, we can't take our broomsticks—we have to walk.

What Happens If...?

 **THE STORY**

Dorothy is just about to leave Munchkinland to travel to the Emerald City in search of the great and powerful Wizard of Oz.

Glinda
It's always best to start at the beginning—
and all you do is follow the Yellow Brick Road.

Dorothy
But—what happens if I—

Glinda
Just follow the Yellow Brick Road.

THE LESSON

Glinda gives Dorothy a direction, and Dorothy immediately has a question that she feels compelled to ask. What happens if . . . ?

Our minds work so quickly, they can instantly imagine potential obstacles. It's a part of our brains' function to analyze and make sense of all incoming information. We are always trying to see and plan for the possible dangers and pitfalls before they occur.

I can't tell you what Dorothy's question was, but I have a feeling it was something along the lines of, "What happens if I get lost?" "What happens if I can't find my way?" "What happens if I run into the Witch?"

I can assure you she wasn't thinking, "What happens if I stumble upon a plane, complete with pilot and free cocktails, and get whisked back to Kansas?" And she wasn't thinking, "What happens if I meet Prince Charming, fall madly in love and never want to leave Oz?" Have you ever noticed that "What happens if" tends to be followed by a negative thought?

What would our attitudes be like if we changed all those negative "what happens ifs" into positive thoughts, trying to imagine good possible outcomes of the situations in our lives?

Whenever I get on a plane, the usual "What happens if we crash?" scenario runs through my brain. And all the lovely images that accompany that—assuming the crash position, being paralyzed by pure panic, ultimately becoming a charred mass of airborne flesh (eeeeeew)—that will lead to my very own funeral, closed casket, of course. Oh jeez, what depressing ruminations, all arising from one little question.

The unfortunate thing is that these thoughts are not limited to when we travel on planes. There are little negatives and "what happens ifs" that occupy our thoughts on a daily basis, and we don't even notice them.

WHAT HAPPENS IF . . . ?   57

They might not be as horrific as the plane scenario, but they affect our moods without our realizing it.

The next time I fly, as soon as my brain turns to "What happens if," those words will be followed by, "the flight miraculously leaves on time and picks up a jet stream so that we arrive a half hour early and my bags are the first two on the conveyer." Yes, that is a much better thought, and it makes me smile. Either scenario probably will not happen, but the latter is so much more enjoyable than imagining terror at thirty thousand feet.

"What happens if . . ." can automatically transport us to a negative frame of mind. Mostly based on fears and the unknown, it is no more real than imagining something pleasant, or the ideal way an event might transpire. Once we are in our negative mode, we sometimes stay there, taking the defensive position on life.

Better to focus on the task at hand. Better to take seriously the flight attendant's pleasantry and "enjoy your flight." Or to follow directions like Glinda's advice, "Follow the Yellow Brick Road," than to open the door to "what happens if . . . ?" We'll never know what happens if, because it will happen the way it's going to happen. It will unfold before our very eyes, and we will experience it. "What happens if . . . ?" is always a moot question.

But what happens if I always follow "What happens if?" with some amazingly great supposition? Perhaps a more positive, worry-free life that might ultimately make me a happier person. What happens if I stay that way?

Follow the Yellow Brick Road

 **THE STORY**

It is a bright, bright, sunshiny day, and Dorothy and the little furball who got this whole story into motion are taking the Munchkins' and Glinda's advice. They are following the Yellow Brick Road, when two roads diverge in the yellow brick. Dorothy, in a quandary, stands a moment and contemplates.

Dorothy
Now which way do we go?

THE LESSON

The paths we take in life are like the Yellow Brick Road.

We could look at our lives as one long *Wizard of Oz* movie, with a beginning, middle and end. Or we could break our lives up into vignettes, each with its own story. Our first love, our first heartbreak, our first time living away from home—all have their own tales, and looking back on them, we can see the twists and curves of the road. The forests that we trudged through and the wicked witches we had to battle. Our jobs, our families, our health issues, our friendships, our spirituality, and the list goes on—every aspect of our lives has its own path.

And just as we can look at our past, right now we are traversing down one of the many Yellow Brick Roads of our lives. So where are you on the Yellow Brick Road of your career? Your spiritual practice? How about your highway of love?

You can look at almost any conflict in your life as its own mini-movie. And, as in any movie, the heroine needs to do something. In this case, Dorothy needs to choose a path. At a time of decision, we are just like Dorothy staring blankly at the two paths in front of her. This way or that way? We have no idea which path would be better. We can't see into the future. We might be able to make some educated guesses or narrow it down to the pros and cons of a particular question.

We research. We contemplate. We weigh all the factors. What happens when, after all that time pondering, we still don't know what to do? Do we flip a coin? Just not choose? Sometimes, not choosing is a choice.

We've all probably passed up an opportunity because of not being able to make up our minds. *Oz* would be a pretty boring movie if Dorothy plopped her stuff right down and set up camp in the middle of the fork because she just couldn't decide which way to go.

We all have been there—in the land of limbo trying to determine where the hell we need to go and hoping that, oh my gosh, we choose correctly. We lose sleep, we worry, we ruminate, trying to gain some insight into where each path will take us. Ugh! The pressure. We don't want to make a bad decision.

We ask everyone we know to give us their two cents, and then we are completely paralyzed. People we love and respect can give us good advice, and it doesn't hurt to consider it. Their suggestions are often based on how they would react in a similar situation. If they are not risk takers, their advice will be more conservative. If they are bold, they might point us in a different direction. Every opinion they offer will have behind it their entire life experience. Know that you can get input, but only you can decide which path you will take.

The idea of the "right" thing to do is a deceptive one. The secret to any decision, no matter how huge, is knowing there is no one right answer. They are all right decisions. Your path is your path, and you will get to where you want to go.

Glinda told Dorothy all she had to do to find the Wizard was to "follow the Yellow Brick Road," so both roads led to the Emerald City. If Dorothy had taken the other route, we would have had an entirely different movie. One path might have been shorter, and she might have met a snuffleupagus instead of a lion, but either path would have eventually landed her smack-dab in front of those emerald gates.

In our lives it's the same thing—all we can do is make a choice and start walking. If halfway down the path we don't like it, it dead-ends, or it doesn't look so good, we can always turn back or try to find a shortcut.

Sometimes we choose path A, and it doesn't turn out the way we planned. Maybe our Yellow Brick Road turns into a brown dirt trail, barely visible and all uphill. As we trudge up our hill, with every agonizing step, we wish we had taken B.

We can create big stories around B. That path would have been so wonderful and amazing, a path all downhill—filled with roses and a nice, pretty stream. Soon we can despise the path we're on, which we've started to liken to our own personal hell while envisioning B as some utopia we'll never visit.

The truth of the matter is we don't, or won't, ever know what path B was like—we didn't take it. Who's to say it wasn't just as rocky as our path, or maybe even steeper?

Try not to focus on the path you didn't take but, rather, on where you are and where you are going. You, like Dorothy, are making your way as best you can. You are experiencing a new chapter to add to the story of your life. Whatever you are doing, know that wherever you want and need to go, you'll get there, as long as you keep moving forward. Choose and go forth boldly. All paths lead to the Emerald City—one path isn't better than another, just different.

No Brain?

Dorothy is at a fork in the Yellow Brick Road, and there, suspended in the middle of a cornfield, is a friendly scarecrow. Dorothy, being the kind-hearted soul that she is, helps him down, and they get to chatting. Dorothy finds out that the Scarecrow is missing a vital organ: He has no brain. What he lacks upstairs, he more than compensates for in the singing and dancing department, which he demonstrates though his fine ditty, "If I Only Had a Brain."

THE LESSON

I don't know about you, but "If I only had a brain" could definitely be my motto every time I do something without really thinking about it and the result leaves me shaking my head in disbelief. Take, for example, the inconvenience of locking my keys in the car and the much bigger woe of dating the wrong person for way too long. These markedly different scenarios have in common the absence of thought—one for just an instant and the other for quite some time.

The expression (often muttered by my father) "I'd lose my head if it weren't screwed on" illustrates just how frequently we are like the Scarecrow and completely stop thinking.

The Scarecrow sings about what he would do if he had a brain. During his song, he says he'd be able to sit and ponder and think, and perhaps solve problems of troubled people in the world. He has hopes and dreams of what he would do if he just had the mind for it.

Now, I have to confess that our friend the Scarecrow would be disappointed with my brain usage. Sitting around and pondering don't usually make it onto my To Do list. Who has the time? My life is hectic, with not a minute to spare—working crazy hours at a job I'm not thrilled about that stresses me out constantly. After work, there's a lot to cram in—exercising, answering e-mail, doing laundry, cleaning, walking the dog, grocery shopping, paying bills, and on it goes. No matter how hard I work at my life, it always feels like I'm playing catch-up—and, like a hamster on a wheel, no matter how quickly I run, I'll never get there. And it is usually during this sort of hamster frenzy that I leave my wallet someplace strange or miss an important lunch meeting.

When your brain is out to lunch instead of you, it is actually trying to get your attention. It is in these instances that you should do as the Scarecrow would: Take a time-out, reenergize your brain, think and reflect.

In this technologically advanced world, our time to pause, without the distraction of the TV or something dinging or ringing, is almost never. And because we are always connected to other things, we are not as plugged into our own lives.

Sitting quietly or meditating can keep us more in tune with ourselves. If meditating is not for you, you can take a leisurely stroll down the street, or plant yourself in the comfiest chair in the house, put on a mellow CD and just chill out. Whatever allows you to stop, clear your mind and get centered. Just by sitting calmly, you'll be able to feel all the hustle and bustle and stress of life falling away.

This space is where the wisdom within you lies. This is the place where all inspiration emanates from, where great thoughts begin and where miracles and transformation occur.

In this place you can get in touch with how you are doing. Ponder your life a bit, and ask yourself some questions. How am I feeling today? What should I focus on this week?

How often do you really contemplate the hard questions? What is my purpose? How am I contributing to others? Am I happy? What would I need to do if I decided to do something different? Is my life meaningful? What is my most self-destructive fault? What does this disappointment mean? What is the lesson here? What do I need to change in order to improve my life? Your brain has all the answers to those big questions—if you want to know them.

That, I guess, is the scariest part. Once you start to ask yourself these questions, you sometimes get answers that you might not want to hear.

What happens when you ask yourself about your day-to-day work? Does this fulfill me? Does this serve my life in a positive way? Is this what I should be doing? Does this job have room for advancement? When you dig a little deeper to get a course of action, like going back to school, or looking for a job with another company (something new and unknown), it seems downright frightening. But trust your inner wisdom: It tells you what you need to know, and you'll know when it's an absolute truth. Even if it leaves you white-knuckled about your life, not to worry—big changes don't need to happen overnight. Your brain is also there to help you mull it over, work through it and make things happen when you are ready for them.

The more we check in with ourselves, the more we will pay attention to that inner wisdom. We've all had those instances when we hear that little singsongy voice chirp, "You should not be doing this." Or, "This is not a good idea." Then later we find out it was right, and we are so annoyed with ourselves. Why didn't we listen to it? Was it a self-destructive act? Was it avoidance? Did we ignore that warning from ourselves in order to be happy for an instant? (We all know how shortsighted that can be.) These are questions to be asking ourselves so that we don't repeat mistakes. If we can start to follow our own mindful and well-thought-through directions from that centered place, it will lead us to experiencing greater good in our lives.

Your brain is ultimately there to illuminate your perfect path. What would happen if you let your brain out, let it imagine your life and the way you would like it to be? Let it tell you new thoughts. Let it be your resource. It just might blow your mind to see what sort of answers you get. If you are open to it, it will help you accomplish things you never even dreamed possible.

Instead of looking for answers outside ourselves, we need to remember to take the time to get centered and use our brains the way the Scarecrow would—for problem solvin' and ponderin'. Consult the inner wisdom contained within your noggin.

It's Hip to Skip

 **THE STORY**

After the Scarecrow sings his fine song about needing a brain, Dorothy is very impressed and asks him to go with her to see if the Wizard of Oz can help him out in the noggin department. He thinks (well, if he could, anyway) it's a fine idea, and off they go skipping down the Yellow Brick Road.

THE LESSON

Dorothy leaves Munchkinland skipping. She meets the Scarecrow, and they get to skipping. With each person she meets, it's skipping, skipping and more skipping.

It is with great irony that I sit down to write this chapter with a broken toe. Ah, the days of skipping have left me for a while. I remember them fondly. Do you?

You know, the time when going to your best friend's house required a leisurely skip down the street. The wind in your hair, the up-and-down glide of a skip, was so fun. Expending lots of youthful energy while at the same time getting where you needed to go twice as fast as walking.

Now that we are all grown up, we just don't skip. The skip in us has died, my friends, and it's up to us to revive it.

Why skip? Exercise! It's a full-body exercise and good for you! Why waste your money on your membership at the gym when you can skip those thighs away for free? It's a great way to get your rear and legs in shape. It's faster than a walk and slower than a jog, but it still gets your heart rate going. You can burn double the calories you do when you are walking, and it's a lower-impact exercise, so it's easier on your body.

Besides, skipping can make you feel happier and lighter. Next time you're harried and rushing down the street, try skipping just halfway down the block. You'll find your mood altered—you'll be in a happier frame of mind.

What will the neighbors think? Who cares? Why are you trying to impress them? They will probably think, "There she goes, skipping," and it'll make them smile. Just think, you can make tons of people smile wherever you go, and get exercise. I have visions of a day when all the wisecracking, tough-talking New Yorkers decide they've had it with walking and skip through Times Square.

I dream of a day when skipping becomes a normal part of life for grown-ups, just like eating bran cereal and talking about losing those last ten pounds. "Honey, sorry I'm late. But I was skipping down Fourth and ran into Susan from work. We skipped down to Eighth to grab some coffee." I want it to be commonplace for the exercisers of America to say, "Hey, what are you doing later? Want to go skipping?"

But seriously, why don't we skip anymore? Isn't it sad? Skipping is not the only thing we might have forgotten; there's also what it represents: the whimsical, fun part of ourselves. The free spirit that used to skip when it wanted to. Remember that part of you that used to spin in place just to feel the sensation of dizziness, the part that did handstands to see how many seconds it could stay upside down? We used to make strange noises and faces whenever we felt like it. As kids, we used to do whatever inspired us, and now we have conformed to doing only what is appropriate. We are old and boring and far too serious for our own good sometimes.

Where did those little kids in us go? Don't worry, they're still in there; to find them, we just might have to put a skip in our step.

No Heart?

THE STORY

Dorothy and her new pal the Scarecrow happen upon a rusted-frozen Tin Man. Dorothy finds an oilcan nearby, and she tends to the stuck parts. He's almost as good as new but still not quite right—the absent-minded tinsmith did not give him a heart. He dances his silvery self around and sings about what he would do if he had a heart.

THE LESSON

The Tin Man needs a heart, and in this story he represents the need for love.

Love is a quality that's almost impossible to describe. I looked it up in my dictionary, and it says, "A strong affection for someone or something."

I guess that definition works when you say, "I love chocolate," or, "I love the movie *The Wizard of Oz*."

Sitting here thinking about the love I feel for God, my family, my significant other, my dog and my life, I know the above definition falls short. I can't imagine my guy looking deeply into my eyes and saying, "I have a strong affection for you." (It sounds like he has trouble expressing his feelings.) It doesn't come close to the meaning of love.

The love I am talking about is the universal emotion, the sacred aspect of love, and not just the flippant word that many toss around carelessly like a Frisbee. Love is the most powerful emotion. Love is that magical quality that makes us feel complete. Love can neutralize hate, overcome fear and demolish sadness. It is the universal thread that can connect us all. Love is the emotion that, when we feel it, makes everything else pale in comparison.

We all have the need for love. Whether we give it or receive it, love fuels our lives. If we are experiencing love, our lives are transformed, not just in the physical world but in our souls.

A lot of people feel like the Tin Man—that they do not have love in their lives. Many different kinds of love exist: romantic love, parental love, friendly love and self-love, to name a few. They all stem from the same place—an ultimate appreciation, a boundless goodwill and a never-ending compassion.

Our culture has placed romantic love on a higher pedestal than the other kinds of love. Being in a romantic relationship, finding that movielike bliss with someone, is the sought-after prize. Unfortunately, all too much emphasis is placed on finding that one special person in order to feel love, and it is often talked about as a prerequisite to our own happiness.

The Tin Man has taken the right approach: He knows it is something he is lacking within himself that he needs to find in order to experience all kinds of love. To get love, you have to feel love first. If you want someone to love you, you have to love yourself first. (Ugh—we hear that all the time. But really, it's true.)

Love is an attitude of pure good intentions and kindness toward everything and everyone in your life (including yourself). Giving that emotion out at all times is a pretty tall order. We love certain people, and others not so much. We love certain parts of ourselves, and other parts we can't stand. We love some aspects of our lives but are resentful of others.

Many times when we are unhappy, angry, confused or upset, it's because, just like the Tin Man, we have lost our connection to our hearts. At these times we can focus on the love in our lives. If we are blue, we might focus on the people who love and care for us. If we are unhappy about specific circumstances, we can focus on and appreciate the things and experiences that are good in our lives. If we are in a fight with someone, we can take a time-out from our anger and remember what we love about them. If everything we do radiates from that center within us that can tap into our feelings of wholeness and warmth, then even though circumstances are not exactly what we think they should be, in our hearts we can know that our lives are an amazing gift, and we will make our way out of difficult emotions and situations more easily.

Love is like a universal slot machine. (In this casino, the odds are always in your favor.) But just as with any slot, you need to start feeding it before you can get your jackpot. The only coins that this machine takes are tokens of love, and any good deeds, well wishes and generous actions will be accepted. A nice thought, an encouraging word or a random act of kindness—this machine does not care what kind of love coin you put into it. You just need to start feeding it.

Once you begin loving first, the slot machine gets into a groove with you and your life. Life showers you with surprises. A compliment out of the blue, a kind word from a stranger, or perhaps an unexpected gift. Once you put some love out there, love will make its way back to you. This love is within us, and it's ours to give as well as receive. We can't stop it once it starts. We can just try to give more and more—the more we give, the more we get back.

What does it mean to love as much as you can? It means to approach everything you do with a benevolent heart—whether it's standing in line at the post office or having a disagreement with a friend. If you can have that attitude in all your daily activities, your life will become more fulfilling.

You know when you are not being loving, when you are being bitchy or mean or just not nice. You can ask yourself in tough moments, "Am I being loving?" You can express all your feelings with a loving heart. You can tell someone you are mad or hurt with love in your heart—it will just be expressed in a much nicer way and help resolve conflicts better.

For one day you can decide to be more loving and see what happens. Maybe there's one person and one relationship you want to focus on. No matter what the interaction, remember to focus on that center of love in your heart.

This love will fuel you, it will get you out of yourself, and it will change your life. Remember, the more time we spend loving, the more the casino gives us back. It's Love Vegas. Okay, so maybe the slot machine is a silly analogy, but it's true. Once we start infusing our lives with love, we find out that the ability to experience love is within us all the time.

The Tin Man starts down the path with Dorothy in search of a heart, but during his journey they become friends, and that is when he starts to love. He has allowed a relationship with another person to blossom. He has put time and energy and emotion into his friendship, and it has grown into love.

Love connects each person on this earth to another person, no matter how lonely or scared or fragile. When you feel like the Tin Man, all empty and hollow, remember that the love we are seeking starts with us. Have a heart, and love.

Should I Stay or Should I Go?

 **THE STORY**

Dorothy and the Scarecrow decide it would be a good idea to ask the Tin
Man along.

Dorothy

You know, we were just wondering why
you couldn't come with us to
the Emerald City to
ask the Wizard of Oz for a heart.

Tin Man

Well, suppose the Wizard wouldn't
give me one when we got there?

THE LESSON

The Tin Man's simple question is an honest one. When starting off on a new scary adventure to see a Wizard, one wants to be sure that the journey will be worth it—that the time, the skipping, the blisters, the long, long trek, will pay off.

It sounds reasonable to want to know up front if the result will be a good one. For who would travel on purpose down a path that will lead to a dead end? The problem with any good, serious journey is that the future is uncertain. The dreams we are chasing are always going to be big. The stakes may be high. The things we want may exceed our grasp, but grasp away, I say!

It's easier said than done. Because a lot of the time we think like the Tin Man. "I could go all the way to Oz and return with no heart? Forget it!" But as with any quest, the outcome is never guaranteed. If we are making big changes, or taking chances, to achieve something greater in our lives, the proposition of no guarantees does not seem very appealing.

Sometimes it's easier to stay where we are—in a job that is unfulfilling; or in a relationship that's terrible but better than being alone; or at home, safe, comfortable, on the couch with cookies, watching TV. We know the outcome of that choice, and we trick ourselves into thinking we are okay with it. It's easier to do what we've been doing, and it's hard to make a change and do something new, no matter how unhappy we are with the status quo. Change is scary, but we must press on.

To not go down a path because of an uncertain result is not an empowering choice and will ultimately backfire. Not to follow our hearts (or, in this case, search for one) because we are not sure where it will lead will only keep us where we are. If we don't pursue what we want, we will not progress. Our lives will be the same, and for a while we might feel comfortable, but after a time, our spirits will long for something more.

We all have a need to bring new experiences into our lives, to have the excitement of trying to go beyond our capabilities and of doing things we never dreamed possible. If we don't try it, we will be left with an empty, blah feeling, a disenchantment with our lives in general, and not know what to do with it. The longer we stay stationary, the harder it is to get going.

Regardless of the outcome, a good motivating thought that can help you decide what to do is to ask yourself, "How will I feel if I don't try to do this right now? How will I feel about it ten years from now?" Failing is never a great option, but even if your plans don't work out, you will be filled with a sense of pride and be able to say, "I gave it my best shot—at least I tried."

The things our spirits beckon to us to do are sometimes not about the result at all. Making the journey is what is important. Just making the decision to make the journey can be the lesson we need to learn. Perhaps we'll learn how to deal with complications along the way. Either way, any sojourn will leave us with new experiences and insights. We'll be more equipped for the next time we decide to take a risk. Ideally, the result of taking any great chance will find you someplace better than you had hoped, with an amazing outcome that you never could have imagined at the start of your trek.

The Tin Man would never have found his heart and three new friends if he had decided just to hang out and keep chopping wood. The Tin Man would tell you that his journey was worth it. When we are faced with a challenging new direction, with an unknown result, the only time we fail is when we don't try.

Stand by Your Friends

THE STORY

As the Scarecrow, the Tin Man and Dorothy are about to make their way down the Yellow Brick Road, the Wicked Witch of the West appears. She attempts to scare Dorothy and discourage the Tin Man and the Scarecrow from helping her out. A fireball materializes in the Witch's hand, and she throws it at the Scarecrow. Luckily, it misses. Though visibly shaken by the incident, the two promise Dorothy that they'll protect her and make sure she sees the Wizard—no matter what. She tells them they are the best friends a girl could ask for.

THE LESSON

The Tin Man and the Scarecrow are an awe-inspiring example of how to act when your friends are in a jam. They assure her that the Witch is nothing to worry about. They are not just tagging along to get something they want; they are committed friends of Dorothy's, and they promise to help her get to the Emerald City.

When our friends are having problems (no matter how big, green or ugly), we can start by assuring them that they will get through it. It is sometimes hard to see the proverbial light at the end of the tunnel, especially in the middle, so our encouragement can allow them to see that glimmer. Words of confidence and support take away the helplessness and hopelessness and replace them with strength to face a situation.

The Scarecrow and the Tin Man are there for Dorothy and are sympathetic to her plight. Friends are fun to be around when their lives are stress-free and simple. When a crisis arrives, they might not always be as nice and easygoing. All of us react to problems differently, and our friends are no exception. Depending on their situation, be it a breakup or an illness, their outlook and moods may be a tad altered, and therefore we need to try to be compassionate, try to avoid a tiff and be understanding when perhaps they act harshly. They might not even be reacting to us but to the stress and weight of their predicament.

Lastly, like the Scarecrow and the Tin Man, we should let our friends know that they do not have to go it alone. We are ready and willing to help get them through to the other side of their problem.

As true friends, we will help out whenever and wherever it's necessary. We will listen, and we will be supportive. We'll let them cry on our shoulder, and we'll tell them it's going to be all right. We'll offer a clear perspective. We will shower them with unconditional love and support until the end of time. We'll do whatever they need us to do, and gladly.

We know when we have problems of witchy proportions, our friends will do the same for us. Don't just stand by your man; stand by your friends, even through tough times.

Lions and Tigers and Bears! Oh, My!

 **THE STORY**

Dorothy and her two new friends, the Scarecrow and the Tin Man, skip down the Yellow Brick Road. They follow the winding path, and soon they are engulfed by a spooky forest.

Dorothy
I don't like this forest! It's—it's dark and creepy!

Scarecrow
Of course, I don't know,
but I think it'll get darker before it gets lighter.

Dorothy
Do—do you suppose we'll meet any wild animals?

Tin Man

Hm, we might.

Scarecrow

Animals that—that eat straw?

Tin Man

Some—but mostly lions and tigers and bears.

Dorothy

Lions?

Scarecrow

And tigers?

Tin Man

And bears.

Dorothy

Lions and tigers and bears! Oh, my!

All Three

Lions and tigers and bears!

Dorothy

Oh, my!

THE LESSON

Lions and tigers and bears, oh, my—what a strange ecosystem they have in Oz.

Has this ever happened to you? Somebody says something and you believe it's true, and then you start to get all worked up about it. Can you say Y2K?

The best example of the lions and tigers and bears phenomenon is the local news. Cell phones cause brain cancer! The killer bees are here! A murderer could be living next door! Cell phones and killers and bees, oh, my! It's a wonder anyone leaves the house.

The nightly news has become a gruesome, sensationalized way for the TV stations to get ratings rather than a useful update on the day's pertinent events. Many of the reports we receive are merely speculation, with barely a fact to fall back on. It's exactly like the question, "Do you think we might meet any wild animals?" The answer is that you might, so prepare for the worst!

It's good to be informed, but it's also good to question what, specifically, was presented before reacting. Before becoming panicked, it's helpful to try to see if you can find evidence to dispute the fear. Had Dorothy, the Tin Man and the Scarecrow not gotten frightened, they might have realized it would be three of them against one wild animal. Did they remember that they had an ax (carried by the Tin Man)? Did Dorothy remember that Glinda had given her the ruby slippers and she would be safe? None of that was thought through rationally. They went straight into being scared.

This is what we need to be aware of—the fear-filled perspective that creeps into our thinking without our even knowing it. Daily, we are bombarded with things to be afraid of. It's no wonder we jump to fearful conclusions about what could happen to us. Instead of reacting immediately with the emotion of fear, we need to question the information given and analyze it rationally.

The news is always focusing on death and how to avoid it. The fact of the matter is the average life expectancy is now about seventy-seven years.[1] They really wouldn't have much to say or do if every night they reported, "Welcome to the evening news. You'll probably live to be around seventy-seven, and now here's the sports." They need it to sound dramatic to make sure we'll tune in, and by threatening death and danger, they get our attention.

Be wary of statistics. Many companies finance studies and are reporting statistics that might help them to profit. (Like pharmaceutical companies.) Often, the numbers quoted do not give you the facts about how they came to these conclusions. How many people were tested? Who performed the research? How long did it last? Statistical analysts could tear apart many of these findings to prove them slanted to a certain outcome. Much of the time the newscasters report that "experts say. . . . " Who are these experts? And why aren't they quoting them directly?

If there are no statistics quoted, then you should also be skeptical—is this danger one person's opinion? Is the situation being reported commonplace? The news reports on every single airplane incident as if it were a story. Worldwide, there are over twenty thousand passenger flights a day, and every once in a while things go wrong—the planes turn back, they lose cabin pressure. But is this news? If you lost the air-conditioning in your car, would they find it newsworthy? Probably not, but because it's an airline, they call it news.

We need to be careful not to allow fear to affect the way we live. It's not just the news. It's easy to be influenced by those around us. The workplace is a veritable woods of rumors, gossip, conjecture and speculation. Misinformation spreads like wildfire at work. Imagine this: Tomorrow you say to someone in a hushed tone, "I've heard that we're going to have to work on [insert closest paid holiday name here]." By noon, people will be drafting memos to the president of the company. Why is that? Sometimes people are quick to jump on the lions and tigers and bears bandwagon without checking out the facts.

Friends and family can feed us false and fearful ideas as well. My friend grew up with a mother who was always worried. She was highly intelligent and very well informed. She was consumed with watching the news and reading the paper. She read books constantly, and it seemed she remembered everything she had read, watched and heard. Each day would bring a new fear, something to be watched out for. She was a walking encyclopedia of information, but it always came from worry, doom and gloom. Too much information can be a bad thing, and just because we are imparted facts doesn't mean we have to respond or react to them.

Every time you hear something that might send you into a panic, try to make a case for the opposite. Sure, someone may have been murdered, but did you know that the murder rate in the year 2005 was actually the same as it was in 1966?[2] (Ever hear that on the news?) And that the violent-crime rate in the United States was lower in 2005 than it was in 1975?[3]

As soon as you find yourself becoming afraid of something you've heard, ask yourself, "Is this really true? Is this something that is potentially dangerous in my life? Is this a fact? Do I need to address this, or is this just something to get worked up about?" If you're still unsure, do your own research to make sure the threat actually applies to your life before buying into it.

Most of the time we can be assured that we should not believe the hype!

Don't get sucked into the panic vortex. Just as in our Oz story, panic is contagious and often unfounded. Unless you are a zookeeper, lions and tigers and bears are not what you should worry about. It's news flashes, scare tactics and rumors, oh, my!

No Courage?

THE STORY

As Dorothy, the Scarecrow, the Tin Man and Toto tentatively skip along, the worst thing that was feared, a lion, leaps out of the forest. He appears to be ferocious and quite a bully as he runs after Toto. Dorothy immediately intervenes and stops the Lion with a fine smack on the nose. His growly façade crumbles and he becomes a simpering wimp of a lion, afraid of his own shadow. He's ashamed because he doesn't have one smidgen of courage. He sings "If I Only Had the Nerve," expressing his longing to be the Lion he was born to be—King of the Forest.

THE LESSON

The Cowardly Lion gives new meaning to the term "fraidy cat." In the Oz story he represents that part of us that lives in fear and has the need for courage.

A lion is supposed to be fearless, but instead he is afraid of every-thing. It's no wonder he feels like a failure—he is not fulfilling his pur-pose in life. Like the Lion, we all have a purpose, and whatever fears we have may keep us from living up to our potential.

What can I say about fear? We are all fearful of something. It could be a phobia, like being afraid of spiders or heights. Or it could be some-thing deeper, like a fear of intimacy, a fear of failure or a fear of conflict. We could fear people, places or planes. I can't imagine a person without fears. I am waiting to meet someone who has a fear of being afraid (phobophobia).

The Lion has discovered that being fearful all the time is his biggest obstacle to becoming a great and powerful lion. Just as with the Lion, our barriers to living great and powerful lives are our fears. If we can recog-nize our fears, then we can start to deal with them, and once we begin working to get rid of them, doors of opportunity open up, and our lives are transformed.

Once we've pinpointed a fear, we can try to figure out how it started. Some people have a fear of dogs, and it can usually be traced back to a childhood incident. Some people have a fear of commitment, or rela-tionship fears, that can be linked to their parents' divorce or to their emotional rearing. Finding the origin of fear proves that at one time we lived without this fear, which makes it easier to grasp the idea of getting rid of it.

Maybe your fear can't be traced to something specific, but it is there just the same. Fear, according to the dictionary, is "an anxiety caused by real or possible danger." Whether the fear is real or not, it feels the same. To the person who is afraid of spiders, the fear is very real. No fear, no matter how small, strange or huge, is silly.

A lot of our fears are like being afraid of the bogeyman. The bogey-man is real to a five-year-old. Just as that crying, scared kid needs to be

held and told there's no such thing as the bogeyman, we need to be able to reassure ourselves that our fears, however real they seem, are products of our imaginations. If you can accept this premise, usually you can talk yourself around to the rational side of your mind. Why do you have this fear? What would result if the thing you fear happened? Can you try to deal with it?

People think courage is the absence of fear, but I would argue that courage is the ability to stand up to your fears and act in spite of them. Without fear, how could we ever be courageous? We can have fear, but once we push past it, that is when the miracles happen.

Fears are just thoughts in our mind, mostly of our own creation, and the best way to deal with them is to prove them wrong. My friend was deathly afraid of heights, and one day we were watching a TV show with sky divers. She told me that she dreamed of confronting her fear of heights by jumping out of a plane. She said she had a feeling it just might change her life. I thought if she felt that way, then she should do it. Since it was on my list of things to do someday, I told her I'd go, too. (Immediately after opening my big mouth, I was terrified.) Two days later, we jumped out of a plane (attached to skydiving instructors who do this all the time, of course).

Even with an expert on your back, nothing you have ever done in your life can prepare you for the moment when you are up there, twelve thousand feet in the air, and they yank open the door to the plane. You look down at all the little squares that represent miles of acreage, and you take a deep breath and leap into the unknown. It was an amazing and terrifying experience. Even if you aren't afraid of heights, it's an experiment in courage.

My friend is a perfect example of someone who looked her fear straight in the eye and defied it. She says that her life has been transformed and her fears are minimal. Now, anytime something scares her or seems impossible, she says to herself, "I jumped out of a plane—this will be easy." It is her motivating mantra that now fills her with courage.

Courage is a deep inner strength that allows us to know that no matter what happens, we are going to be okay. It is not only an inner strength but also a willingness to put ourselves in uncomfortable and possibly risky situations to work through these fears. Why must we conquer them? Well, for starters, it's no fun sitting around being afraid.

Jumping out of an airplane to conquer fear is not for everyone, but being determined to work through the fear is the key to getting rid of it. Staying focused on eliminating the fear and trying to confront it little by little each day is a formula for success. If you are afraid of spiders, try killing one instead of running away screaming, then try to work up to catching one and letting it go free. (Who knows, someday you might want a pet tarantula.) Devise a plan to deal with your fear and whittle it down week by week.

These are by no means the correct or only solutions to your fears, just simple ideas to help you get started. There are books and people aplenty that can help you combat your fears. Just to begin dealing with your fears is a huge accomplishment.

Remember the Cowardly Lion, who confronted his fears and went in search of courage. He became the majestic Lion he was meant to be. Do whatever it takes. We are creatures magnificent and splendorous. We do not have the luxury of time, of wasted hyper-anxiety, to sit and worry. We have things to do. We don't want to be afraid. We want to experience the joy and the fullness of our lives. To do this, we must try to fulfill our highest potentials. Are you afraid of it? Yup. Are you going to try to get rid of that fear and blast it into smithereens so all that emerges is that beautiful, radiant, confident, fearless, courageous you? You betcha! Move forward in search of your courage, and try your best to fear less.

Dorothy's Friendships

 **THE STORY**

Dorothy has met the third stranger, the Cowardly Lion, on her way to see the Wizard. She listens to his problem of being a big fat coward. She, of course, asks him to come with her to see if the Wizard can help him out.

THE LESSON

When it comes to being a friend, Dorothy is one person I'd have on my list any day of the week. But darn it, having fictional friends leaves your party pretty sparse when you have one. So I try to learn from her, to know how to be a good friend and to look for real people with Dorothy-like qualities.

From the first second she lands in Munchkinland, Dorothy is the ambassador of nice. She says hello. She is polite. She says please and thank you. She is completely charming at all times.

Wouldn't it be great if everyone were like that? If when they said good morning and asked how you were, they stopped to listen to the answer? Meeting people is an exchange that we often don't pay attention to. Dorothy does it with grace and ease. She speaks to everyone as if they were the most interesting person she has ever met, and they respond accordingly.

Everywhere she goes, she makes friends easily, because she treats every person as if they were already her friend. When we don't know someone, it's easy to be indifferent or not as nice to them as we are to people we know. If we treat everybody like our friends, they'll be friendlier to us.

The best way to do this is to be a good listener. Each person Dorothy meets gets her full attention. She is interested in what they have to say. Each character has a story to tell (in this case, a song to sing). She listens to all of them as they confide in her their biggest problems.

From the second she meets someone, she is helpful. She helped the Scarecrow down from a pole, she oiled the Tin Man, and she wiped the Lion's tears when he was crying. Small gestures of kindness can say volumes.

Once she's listened to a problem, she shares one of her own. "Hey, I know how you feel—I'm lost and I'm trying to go home." Then she tells them what she's doing to try to solve her problem and invites them to come along and maybe get some help too. This is the secret to being a good friend—listening, responding, sharing and offering help if it's needed. She does not try to solve anybody's problem or pretend to know how to; she just offers advice, and they can take it or leave it.

When her friends do something nice, she lets them know she appreciates them. When the Tin Man and the Scarecrow promise to get Dorothy to the Emerald City, she tells them how much it means to her to have such good friends. Everyone needs to hear a compliment every once in a while, and telling your friends how much they mean to you will make your bond even stronger.

Not only does she value them, and their help, but she reciprocates. When the foursome sees the Wizard for the first time (which takes place later on in the story), the Wizard, being so big and powerful, scares the Lion so much that he faints. (I'd faint if I saw a floating head yelling at me.) Dorothy scolds the great and powerful Wizard. She stands up for her friends, even when they can't.

She is completely nonjudgmental. She meets new people, and even though they have faults, she doesn't care. She doesn't mind spending time with someone who's not too smart, or someone who has a hard time loving people, or someone who's a really big wimp. She sees beyond their shortcomings and recognizes the good things about each of her pals. She knows that friends have faults. We all do.

If we see the flaws in others, we can appreciate them as a part of the whole. The friend you love so much would not be the same person without that quality you might consider very unbecoming. The more you embrace people for who they truly are, the more they will embrace you, and then those flaws will become insignificant.

And how does she manage to be such a great friend and make it all seem so effortless? How is it even possible? Well, you need to have love in your heart when it comes to your friends. The unconditional kind is the foundation true friendships are built upon, and everything else—such as anger, disappointment and squabbles—will melt away if you are acting from love.

It's not always easy to do, but if you can, try to be a friend like Dorothy.

Dorothy's Rules of Friendship:

Be nice.

Listen.

Share.

Try to be helpful.

Invite people into your life.

Tell your friends you appreciate them.

Stand up for them.

Be nonjudgmental.

Love them unconditionally.

Off to See the Wizard

THE STORY

Along the Yellow Brick Road our heroes and heroine sing a fine little tune.

All

We're off to see the Wizard,
The wonderful Wizard of Oz.
We hear he is a whiz of a Wiz
If ever a Wiz there was.
If ever, oh ever a Wiz there was
The Wizard of Oz is one because
Because, because, because, because, because
Because of the wonderful things he does.
We're off to see the Wizard,
The wonderful Wizard of Oz.

Dorothy sings this at the start of her journey, and, every chance she gets, she sings it over and over.

THE LESSON

"Off to see the Wizard" could be considered a mantra, a mission statement, a goal or a friendly reminder. Glinda told Dorothy she had to see the Wizard to get back home. Every so often Dorothy reminds herself where she is going and what she is doing.

We are not always as focused as we could be as we attempt to juggle different aspects of our lives. Between work, family, friends, church or synagogue, personal goals, fitness goals, cleaning, cooking, laundry, we are busy every waking second. (Why can't we just extend the day to twenty-eight hours? I'm positive I could get it all done then! But I digress.)

When our day-to-day responsibilities take over our lives, our true desires can get lost. But whatever it is we keep saying we'd like to do, we can make happen. "I'd like to learn to speak Spanish." "I'd like to go back to school." We can focus on one new task and fit it into our lives if we decide to make it important.

Once we have a goal, it's important to remind ourselves daily what we need to focus on in order to carry out our plans. Declaring, "We're off to see the Wizard," or "I'm off to lose ten pounds," can reinforce that goal.

This week I am working on sticking to my diet. "I'm going to be a goddess-like gal and wear a sexy bathing suit." I repeat it ten times to myself in the morning, and every time the temptation for chocolate and potato chips arises, I say my mantra and really let it sink in. My urge to splurge evaporates. (I'm hoping my thighs will, too!) If we can affirm our intentions every morning, we'll be aware of them, and that way we'll have no way to ignore what we need to do. If we don't tell ourselves what to do, it's easy to forget and get sidetracked.

You can use a phrase to accomplish big goals or tiny little ones. Making time each morning to get focused is an empowering way to start your day. Whatever you are off to do, think of your own personal mantra, and repeat it whenever you can to remind yourself of your purpose.

The Field of Poppies

 **THE STORY**

Still singing "Off to See the Wizard," the group turns a corner to find the Yellow Brick Road trails off into a gorgeous field of poppies with the dazzling Emerald City off in the distance. Excitedly, they leap off the path and bound through the poppies, but unfortunately, the Wicked Witch has put a spell on these lovely flowers. Dorothy suddenly becomes overwhelmingly sleepy and lies down to rest, immediately followed by a very drowsy Cowardly Lion.

The Scarecrow and the Tin Man are not affected (being made of straw and tin), except for the fact that they are panicked about what to do with their snoozing pals.

Tin Man
It's the Wicked Witch! What'll we do? Help! HELP!

Scarecrow
It's no use screaming at a time like this!
Nobody will hear you! Help! HELP!

But someone is magically listening—it's Glinda the Good Witch. She breaks the spell with falling snowflakes that wake Dorothy and the Lion. Now back on track, they run all the way to the Emerald City.

THE LESSON

The part of this scene that really gets me smiling is when the Tin Man starts screaming his oil-funnel head off for help. The Scarecrow (even though he feels that shouting out in the middle of nowhere is hopeless) joins in because he has no idea how to get out of this particular jam.

When you are absolutely and completely stuck with nowhere else to turn, you might as well just start using those lungs and bellow for help. The louder the better! Who knows, someone just might hear you and lend a hand.

Asking for help is not always easy. I am the queen of self-reliance, a do-it-yourself kind of person. I would sooner walk to work than ask for a ride. When moving, I'd rather pack everything and hire movers than ask friends for a little free manpower. When I'm throwing a party and people ask what they should bring, I tell them nothing. When the party is over and they ask if they can help clean up, I will not let them lift a finger. At

work I will stay late into the evening (no overtime pay) to get the job done, even if it's twice the workload. I can do it, not a problem.

These may seem like minor examples. They are certainly not of stuck-under-the-spell-of-a-wicked-witch proportions. But I've found that since I'm not accustomed to asking for help with the little things, when it comes to the really critical times, it's even more difficult to ask for help. My tendency is to just not ask for it at all.

This way of behaving is not good. Who the heck do I think I am? Wonder Woman? Somewhere in my crazy brain there's a part of me that thinks that asking for help is like wearing a gigantic sign that says, "I am a wimp and cannot handle my life!" I refuse to walk around like that, and therefore I pretend I can handle it all. Then, when I am exhausted from all of my superhero shenanigans, I become resentful that others aren't more helpful (even though I've never uttered a peep about it).

Where did this phenomenon start? It probably comes from a combination of factors. Perhaps it stems from the attitudes of the fifties, when the men were the breadwinners, with their women at home trying to outdo one another with their Cleaver-ness. The home was a reflection of the woman as a person.

This idea of achievable perfection has been passed down, even though times have changed. We are still trying to project these images, still trying to make sure that others think we are perfect. On some level we still believe that if we ask for help, others will think less of us. But nothing could be further from the truth. Other people are not secretly judging us and thinking that we cannot handle our lives.

A lot of times I do not ask for help because I do not want to inconvenience, burden or upset anyone else with my problems. People like to be helpful; it gives them purpose and allows them to feel useful. And it is in these situations that we become closer to our friends. Accepting help from other people is inviting them to share your life, the good and the bad.

Sometimes you may have nowhere to turn, just like our friends in the field of poppies. If you don't know what to do, ask for help. I assure you that if you sat down in the middle of the street and just started shouting for help, someone would come by, ask what's wrong and try to help you out. I am not suggesting you try this—you would look pretty darn silly, and it's probably not the best way to get out of a jam. The point I am trying to make is that we are only one cry away from the help that we need.

Shouting to the heavens, "Hey, I need a little help here!" is a kind of prayer. If we can acknowledge that we are overwhelmed, it opens the space for the help to come through. Sometimes there are unseen forces at work in your favor, and, just like Glinda, they may send a little aid your way.

Whatever the trouble, if it is more than you can handle, don't be too proud to ask for help. Some kind soul will come to your rescue.

Knock, Knock. Who's There?

THE STORY

Dorothy and friends skip up to the shiny green gates of the Emerald City. They ring the doorbell, and a fine chiming is heard. An odd little gate-keeper appears through a porthole in the door. He tells them to read the notice. Dorothy and pals are confused, as there is no sign posted. The gatekeeper sees the sign is missing, shakes his funny little head and disappears. He comes back, sign in hand, and quickly places it where it should have been. It reads, "Bell out of order. Please knock." They knock, and he answers the door.

THE LESSON

It's a strange moment in the movie, a comical non sequitur. The irony is that the bell was working, and the sign was not needed. This scene is one of my favorites, but it's so short, I wondered if there was even a lesson to be had. Then I remembered a sermon at church with this very scene as a topic. My minister, Marlene, talked one day about how we treat aspects of ourselves just like the bell.

We have things in our lives that are not working. Just as with the bell, we can put a sign on them: If my weight is not working, the sign might read: "I'm fat." Whatever parts of our lives aren't working, we label them "out of order."

Take a statement like "I'm not very smart." Maybe the person who hangs that sign around her neck did not get good grades in high school. Perhaps there was an underlying problem like dyslexia that can explain the bad grades. Or maybe she wasn't motivated or didn't like school, which has no bearing on a person's intelligence. The question now is, is this still true? Is this part of her life still out of order, or is it like the bell at the Emerald City gates?

A lot of our signs were not even hung by us but instead are fundamental beliefs we have about ourselves given to us by our family members. "She's not responsible." "She's lazy." "She's difficult." For some reason, we believed them. But maybe we need to take a closer look. We might not actually be that way. My family had always told me I was irresponsible and wasn't good with money. For years I thought those two statements were fairly accurate.

When I sat down to look at those labels, I suddenly realized they weren't true at all. Was I responsible? I had been living on my own in California, with a steady job, for seven years. I paid my rent on time. No bill collectors were banging on my door. In fact, at my job I was responsible for keeping track of twenty million dollars (as an accountant for a TV show). Now why would they put me in charge of all that money if they thought I was irresponsible? They wouldn't. Just by coming up with examples of how you contradict those labels in your life, you can make them disappear. The list can be so long that by the time you are done, the sign can seem laughable.

Saving my money was also an issue, and I had always believed that sign to be true. It seemed that I lived paycheck to paycheck, with not much money left over, even after getting promotions and raises. I kept telling myself, "I'm a terrible saver," until one day I decided to prove myself wrong and resolved to try to save some money—not a huge, drastic sum but a realistic amount that was automatically deducted from my paycheck each week into a separate account. Over time it piled up—so much that I took some time off to write this book. It feels great to have traded in my "irresponsible" sign for a "very responsible" one and my "can't save a dime" sign for "a great saver when she puts her mind to it."

Check out what negative signs you've been hanging outside your door. Maybe they're not true and you just don't know it yet. We can always challenge those inner beliefs to see if they are incorrect, and perhaps those aspects of ourselves are just like the bell at the Emerald City gates—in perfect working order.

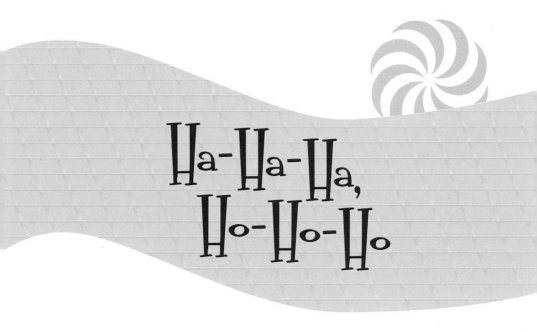

Ha-Ha-Ha, Ho-Ho-Ho

THE STORY

After a bit of chatter, the gatekeeper opens the gates, and our motley group walks into the Emerald City. It is as sparkly green and beautiful as one would imagine. The residents welcome the visitors with a splendid little ditty-and-dance extravaganza. Our characters get cleaned up and ready for their visit to see the Wizard. They sing the snappy "Ha-ha-ha, Ho-ho-ho" song, and the words are sunny and fun. Just in case you missed them:

> *Ha-ha-ha, Ho-ho-ho,*
> *And a couple of tra-la-las.*
> *That's how we laugh the day away*
> *In the merry old Land of Oz.*

THE LESSON

We take life too darn seriously. It's bills and traffic and stress! Oh, my! We act as if everything in our lives is of the utmost importance, when actually most of our daily upsets are just wasted grumpy energy sending us further and further into a deep dark mood.

If you stop to think about it, we are very lucky. Any one of us who is capable of buying and reading this book falls into the category of getting her basic needs met—food, shelter, clothing. The vast majority of us have far more than most of the people in the world.

Knowing this, we can start to put our lives in perspective. We live in the Emerald City of the world. Our problems, even though they appear to be big, are really not, in the grand scheme of things.

Our daily annoyances are things we should just laugh about. Why waste precious energy getting upset, filling your body with stress? Make up your mind when you get up in the morning—sing your favorite cheery song and be determined to have a giggle-filled day.

Pretend you're in Oz. Someone is curt with you, and instead of snapping back, mentally hum the "Ha-ha-ha" song. By making that choice to respond to negativity with a perky thought, you will find that your day will be transformed. Negativity drains us, and each time we are mad or upset or mirror back the negativity thrown in our direction, we lose our battery power. When we laugh or smile, we recharge, and that's what will allow us to keep going and going.

Laughter soothes the soul. Someone said that, and I'm not sure who. It heals the parts of us that are hurting, or at least cheers them up for a while.

If you can't muster a laugh, how about a smile? A smile on your face shines through to the inside. People respond to your smiles and send you joy back. Even if you don't feel like smiling, try it for a day. Decide to say hello to every person you see. The bigger the smile, the better, and see if your blah mood isn't turned around. It's just a matter of practice. You can change your mood from unhappy to happy if you learn to work with it.

Taking ourselves too seriously begins when we are kids. The worst thing in the world when we were six years old was to be laughed at. We were so sensitive and just learning about the world. Everything we didn't know resulted in a gang of bigger kids snickering at us. It made us feel small and stupid. That's why, even as grown-ups, we still find it hard to laugh at ourselves. We don't like to think of ourselves as comical, in a Three Stooges type of way, but sometimes we are.

Laughing at yourself can be the entrance to a whole new way of living. Laugh at your life instead of bemoaning it. Idiotic moments make great stories, even if it was you who was the idiot. Many aspects of our lives can be turned into anecdotes that will entertain people and brighten their day. (Comedians pay their rent this way.)

My grandma was the woman who loved to laugh. Granny Annie's high-pitched cackle could be heard from a block away if she was really going. When she was in her late eighties, her life was not too much to laugh about. Her knees hurt so badly she couldn't walk, she had no short-term memory, and she had so many ailments that she needed constant attention. Her last years were spent in a home filled with other people who were living out their lives in pain and confusion, but somehow, she never lost her willingness to laugh.

Her positive disposition is my inspiration. She'd say, from her wheelchair, which someone needed to push, "At least I can get around. I don't have it so bad." Other days she'd say, "I may be a crazy old bag, but I'm doing just fine." And she would start to giggle.

One day I visited her, and the TV was on. On the screen was a sappy soap opera with two overdressed women who were sobbing. She looked at the screen and said, "Now what's so bad that they're crying about it?

That's crazy." I agreed with her, and then she said, "I'd rather be laughing than crying any day of the week." And then she started laughing right then and there. "Ha-ha-ha! Ha, ha, ha!" That's been my motto ever since.

When things get you down, realize your problems are just minor in the larger scheme of things, think happy thoughts, sing a silly tune, and whenever you can, choose laughter over sadness. With a ha, ha, ha and a ho, ho, ho (and don't forget the tra-la-las), you can laugh the day away, just as they do in Oz.

Have a Spa Day

THE STORY

During the happy-go-lucky "Ha-ha-ha" song, our foursome is whisked away to an Emerald City spa to get tidied up before meeting the Wizard. The Scarecrow gets new stuffing, the Tin Man gets shined, the Lion gets his mane permed and claws clipped, and Dorothy gets her gingham pressed and her hair done. They leave looking like a million. (I am unsure of the currency over the rainbow.)

THE LESSON

The group's transformation only lasts about half of the song, but I just couldn't resist the lesson: After long journeys, after big events—heck, maybe just for no reason at all—have a spa day!

We can get way too caught up in the drudgery of life and forget that we need to take care of ourselves. We are too busy taking care of everything and everyone else. Spa days are amazing, whether you go to a spa for a massage and a facial or have your very own it's-all-about-me day at home.

Where do you find the time for such things? I know it seems that we don't have a second to spare. If we don't make the time for us, then we can become burned out, stressed out and just plain useless. We make time to do the laundry, clean and take care of all those details. We should consider the time to take care of ourselves just as important as our chores.

It's kind of like paying the bills. We sit down every single month to pay the bills to keep things going smoothly. We have to, or the electricity would stop running, and we'd have no phone. Our time for ourselves should be treated like these bills. We need energy to keep going, and if we don't take the time to relax and restore ourselves, we will run out of it. It's easy to forget to do this, but if we were charged a late fee of fifty dollars every month we did not take time for ourselves, we would make, and keep, that appointment monthly.

Pick a day, any day. Clear your schedule—this day is just for you. You could get your hair and nails done. You could book a day at a spa, go in for a massage, relax and hang out in the Jacuzzi and drink yummy fruity water while reading magazines.

You could get everyone out of the house, rent movies, take the longest bubble bath ever and give yourself a facial. Whatever you want to do. It's all about relaxing and rejuvenating yourself.

Once you've done it, I assure you, your schedule will suddenly have room for more of that fun quality time with you. You could even pick a regular day, or set aside one evening a month—just as you would for all those other important events in your date book. It will be something to look forward to, and way more exciting than (insert dreaded chore from last week here).

Dorothy and her pals, at the end of their trek down the Yellow Brick Road, needed a bit of reviving to continue with their quest. The same goes for you. Go on—plan it right now. Get out your calendar and put it in pen! If you follow no other lesson in this book, follow this one! You won't be sorry. You deserve it. I am not only giving you permission, I am demanding that you take just one day this month for you. Have a spa day!

Surrender Dorothy

 **THE STORY**

After visiting the Emerald City spa, our gussied-up friends are on the way to see the Wizard when the Emerald citizens break out in mass hysteria. The Wicked Witch appears overhead on her broom, skywriting in big black pollution-filled letters:

SURRENDER DOROTHY

Dorothy looks worriedly up at the sky.

Dorothy
Dear, whatever shall we do?

THE LESSON

Never Surrender was going to be the theme of this lesson. When the going gets tough, yadda, yadda, yadda. I think that is a good motto, but that's only part of the lesson.

At this point in the journey, Dorothy has traveled a very long way. She's overcome quite a few obstacles already—a scary forest, a fire-throwing witch and a field of poisonous poppies. The Witch's skywriting would, for a normal person, be the very last straw. This is the part where you think Dorothy could have said, "This Witch is after me, and she's never going to leave me alone. This is hopeless."

Dorothy's question "Whatever shall we do?" is comical. Gigantic black letters in the sky seem to hint at one option, but surrendering does not even cross her mind.

She is steadfast in her quest to find the Wizard to get back home, and nothing will thwart her. She is certainly taken aback by this latest turn of events and can feel the pressure from the Witch escalating, yet she still does not even consider the thought.

Having a mindset so focused that you do not think about quitting when obstacle after obstacle is thrown on your path is what makes the difference between getting it done and giving up.

When whatever we are trying to achieve is met with hardships, the tendency is to give up—especially when we have jumped hurdle after hurdle for a long time. We can reach our limit of stress, frustration and setbacks and want to say, "Forget it, this is just too darn hard." The determination to keep going until we meet our goal, or die trying, is the glue that holds our dreams together and will get us through to the end. The challenge is to keep striving until the goal is met, no matter how hard, no matter how much black smoke is blown in our direction.

Even if the odds are against you, even if you can't see what will happen, even if it looks like you are outnumbered, outpowered and outwitched, don't give up on yourself. Persevere with an attitude of power and resolve until you realize your dreams. No matter what you are trying to achieve, never surrender. As a matter of fact, follow Dorothy's lead, and don't even consider it.

King of the Forest

T H E   S T O R Y

Undeterred by the Witch's skywriting, the troupe waits outside the palace of the Wizard. They are all very excited to meet the great Oz and ask for his help.

Scarecrow

Did you hear that? He'll announce us at once!
I've as good as got my brain!

Tin Man

I can fairly hear my heart beating!

Dorothy

I'll be home in time for supper!

Lion

In another hour, I'll be King of the Forest.
Long Live the King!

Then the Lion sings his famous "If I Were King of the Forest" song, in which he tells the group what he would do as the king. At the end of the song, he's been given a makeshift robe and crown, which are the final touches for him to act out his dream of being King of the Forest.

THE LESSON

As he sings his song, the Lion envisions what it would feel like to be King of the Forest and have all the courage in the world. He sings that he would never be afraid, he'd have the respect of other animals, and he would be compassionate.

We see him surrounded with the idea of courage. He stands up straight, he commands our presence, and he's confident and filled with bravery. For a few precious minutes, he has arrived.

The same can be true for us. We can visualize what our lives will be like when we get what we want, be it a new attitude, a new job, some courage or a much larger bank account. Creative imagining can take us out of ourselves and give us a glimpse of who we will become. It is a powerful way to keep us inspired, because we can experience now what we will create later in our lives.

Sometimes if a book is boring, we might turn ahead thirty pages to see if we want to keep reading. Oh, the main character has found a dead body in the house. Knowing there's an exciting turning point a little later on keeps us hooked into reading the book. Imagining what will happen in our lives thirty days or months ahead can keep us motivated and moving toward our goals.

Take a few quiet minutes and relax. Clear your mind. What is it you wish for most? What will your life look like when that happens? What qualities will you have then that you feel you don't have now? Just let your mind experience what you feel you're lacking. Transport yourself into a situation where that quality or goal is realized, and try to experience it fully in a spectacular daydream.

If it's a personal quality you're working on, like the Lion, just close your eyes and try to feel it. How would you feel if you were more courageous? More loving? If you were anger-free? Stress-free? What would a perfect day spent living and expressing that quality be like? Let your thoughts run wild.

If you have a specific goal, it's very easy to envision the end result. For me, a writer, this is a wonderful exercise. When I'm at Barnes & Noble, I imagine my book displayed on the best-seller shelf. What would that feel like? I get a heavy sigh—I feel relieved and quite pleased. Wow. What an accomplishment. My imaginary scenarios (book signings, sitting in that big comfy chair chatting with Oprah) keep me motivated on those days when the realization of my dreams seems so very far away.

Seeing the finished product in your mind's eye is a way of creating the reality of it. With anything, we need to be able to see what we want in order to create it. The Lion is well on his way to courage after having it for a short while during his song. It isn't long before real courage shows up—and stays with him for good. Creative visualization is one of the most powerful tools to keep us motivated and working toward our goal until we start to see results.

Knowing where you want to go is half the battle. Imagining yourself there is like looking into a crystal ball and seeing your own future. Just by doing that, you are already on your way to making it happen.

A Few Kind Words

 **THE STORY**

As soon as the Cowardly Lion sings his King of the Forest song, the guard appears. He has a message from the Wizard, telling them to go away. They are all very upset, especially Dorothy, who starts to cry.

Dorothy
Oh—and I was so happy!
I thought I was on my way home! . . .
Auntie Em was so good to me—
and I never appreciated it.
Running away—
and hurting her feelings.

THE LESSON

Dorothy is upset because she didn't appreciate Auntie Em. That happens to all of us. We can get so caught up in our lives that we don't stop to appreciate the people closest to us.

The list of people who love us, support us and are there for us on a moment's notice is a long one. Because we are so close to them—our family, our friends and our coworkers—it's easy to take them for granted.

Most of the time we think the people in our lives know that we love and appreciate them and are grateful for everything they've done for us. And if they were asked, they would probably say that's true. Even so, they'd enjoy hearing it now and then.

My very best friend (who teaches me daily how to be a great friend) sent me a card not too long ago, and it said: "Happy random appreciation day! Thanks for being my friend." It was the best surprise ever. We should institute a Random Appreciation Day immediately. But then, if we set a date, it wouldn't be random, would it? Well, you get the idea, and I'm sure you will use it accordingly.

Everybody needs to hear kind words. Nice gestures don't have to cost a lot; all it takes is a card, some fresh-baked cookies or a smile. Be as creative as you want to be. You could write a poem or frame a picture of the two of you, or you could go all out and have an appreciation event. Surprise someone you love with a fantastic dinner. Include five minutes of quality time to tell them why you are so very grateful that they are a part of your life.

Whatever you do, just be sure to let the people in your life know how much they mean to you. You don't want to end up like Dorothy, crying and wishing you had told them.

Meeting the Wiz

THE STORY

Dorothy's waterworks move the guard into arranging a meeting with the Wizard. He's a bellowing, grumpy, gigantic floating green head with lots of special effects. They are quite intimidated. He already knows the reason for their visit—to get a heart, some brains, a little courage and a trip home.

Oz's Voice

The beneficent Oz has every intention of granting your requests. . . .
But first, you must prove yourselves worthy by performing a very small task.
Bring me the broomstick of the Witch of the West.

Tin Man

But if we do that, we'll have to kill her to get it.

Oz's Voice

Oz's Voice
Bring me her broomstick,
and I'll grant your requests.

The next time we see them, they are trudging through the Haunted Forest making their way to the Witch's castle.

THE LESSON

(Okay, so the lesson is *not* "Kill whoever you need to, to get what you want." That lesson will be found in my next book, *Lessons from a Wicked Witch*.)

The Wizard of Oz has requested a very small task. (A very small task my you-know-what!) Obtaining the broomstick of the Witch is a seemingly impossible feat, as the Tin Man points out. Go ask the snarling crone who wants your head on a platter for a favor—yeah, that's a killer idea.

But that is pretty much what they decide to do. They need the Wicked Witch's broomstick, so they fearlessly march into the Haunted Forest to find the Witch. They go forth without complaining, whining or pondering what will happen—without hesitation. They've been told what they need to do, and even though the task is enormous, they go for it.

If we could adopt this same acceptance and strategy in our lives, we would be living out our dreams.

When we are faced with big problems, it's only natural for us to slow down and say, "Wait a minute, I need to think this through." That's where we get stuck, because the answer we come up with may be, "That seems too hard," or, "I'm not sure I can do this."

If we know where we want to go, all we need to do is ask what the logical next step is, then take it. If we are willing to listen (to our inner voice or perhaps our inner Wizard) and follow the advice given, no matter how difficult, we will begin to change our lives.

We would not dream of a thing if our spirit did not know that we could accomplish it. The problem is, our spirit is much more adventurous and confident than we are in our day-to-day life. It's one thing to say, "I want a new career," and an entirely different thing to quit the stable life you have in pursuit of that goal. That takes a leap of faith.

It's like skydiving. No one in his or her right mind would do it. Leaping out at twelve thousand feet and seeing tiny squares on the ground, so very far away, with just a pack strapped to your back, is completely illogical. The first time you do it, all your senses leave you, and it's just blind will and gutsy determination that gets you out that door.

Now, in all probability, no one will ever tell you to jump out of a plane, but there are many instances in life when we are faced with great challenges. Our gut will say, "Do this." Our logical minds will retort, "That's crazy! No way!"

Did Dorothy and her pals say, "No way?" Nope. They just kept moving. They took the command and followed it. To get what we want, to follow our dreams and accomplish big things, we will have to fulfill big requests. Will we sit back and whine about how hard it is? Will we complain about how scary it is? Will we stop in our tracks because we are overwhelmed?

Nope. I hate to quote an ad campaign, but Nike said it best: "Just do it."

No matter how huge the tasks in your life seem, don't get intimidated; just do what needs to be done.

Setbacks, Schmetbacks

 **THE STORY**

Dorothy and pals are walking tentatively through the Haunted Forest when the Wicked Witch's army of flying monkeys soars in and attacks. A pack of monkeys trounce the Scarecrow and start tearing his straw body apart. Another group captures Dorothy and Toto and flies them back to the Witch's castle.

The Scarecrow, now reduced to a pile of straw, summons the Lion and the Tin Man.

Scarecrow
Help! Help! Help!

Tin Man
Oh! Well, what happened to you?

Scarecrow

They tore my legs off,

and they threw them over there!

Then they took my chest out,

and they threw it over there!

Tin Man

Well, that's you all over.

Lion

They sure knocked the stuffings

out of you, didn't they?

Scarecrow

Don't stand there talking! Put me together!

We've got to find Dorothy!

THE LESSON

You've got to look out for those flying monkeys—they can really ruin your day. And on certain days it feels like the invisible flying monkeys have interrupted our lives and completely torn our world apart, just as they have done to the Scarecrow.

He is an amicable and resilient character, especially in this moment. We can admire him for his strength and his passion even in the midst of what would appear to be a huge setback.

He's a mess. I've been a mess, have you? When we feel out of sorts, our bodies are just going through the motions, but our minds are all over the place. When we've suffered a grand disappointment, we are reduced to lying around wondering, "How am I going to get it together?"

We've all been in the same place as the Scarecrow. When it happens to us, we can look to him for advice on how to be. After being torn to pieces, he took a brief moment to ask for help and complain ("They tore my legs off, and they threw them . . ."). In the very next moment his thoughts are on helping Dorothy, not on himself.

When an unfortunate event occurs, we can get caught up in the complaining. "How did this happen?" "Poor me, I feel awful." "Life is so unfair," and on and on. We can spend an inordinate amount of time in pity mode, and it seems like once we start to shop there, it's hard to leave the store.

Instead of lamenting our plight and concentrating on our defeats, we should shift our attention and try to get on with whatever we were doing before the setback happened. What is the next step we need to take? This can move us out of despair and into action.

Of course, that's easier said than done if you are upset or depressed. Sometimes you might not know what to do next. Another hint from this story would be to shift your thoughts outside of yourself and see how you might be helpful to others. If you can help someone else, you will get a break from thinking about your problems. After you've stopped focusing on yourself for a while, you will be in a better frame of mind to deal with your own situation.

The Scarecrow doesn't worry about what just transpired. He's already on to the next thing. Dorothy is in trouble, and he has to find her. His last words, paraphrased, are, "Stop talking and get going."

Getting going is the best way to push through any setback, no matter how difficult or disappointing. Take the next step, formulate a new plan, or help someone else, but don't sit around and mope for longer than need be. Setbacks, schmetbacks—just keep moving forward.

As Sand Through the Hourglass . . .

THE STORY

Dorothy and Toto are captives of the Wicked Witch of the West. The Wicked Witch demands the ruby slippers, but unfortunately, they won't come off Dorothy's feet. The Witch has forgotten that the only way they can be removed is if Dorothy is dead. Toto manages to escape, which angers the Witch even more. She prepares to kill Dorothy and turns over a gigantic hourglass. The red sand falls, marking the time Dorothy has left to live.

THE LESSON

Time is a precious and priceless gift. We can only try to use it as best we can. If this were your last day to live, what would you do? Would you keep everything the same? Say the same things you've said? Do the same things you've done?

Time is a lesson we all know about. As children, we had no concept of it. It seemed to our hyperactive little selves that everything moved so slowly, especially if we were in a room with grown-ups. I remember sitting in church for an hour on Sunday, and I swear I was there for a week. Now, as I get older, the time seems to be gradually going by faster and faster. I'm sure you've experienced the weekend time warp. You blink and it's Friday—"Whew, time to relax." Blink again and the alarm clock rings bright and early for Monday morning. What happens to the time? (Damn, must be those aliens again.) And it's not just weekends—sometimes it's years of our lives that were once in the distant future that have turned into our past. (Remember when the year 2000 seemed as if it were eons away?)

As adults, we realize that time is not an unlimited resource—there are only so many hours in the day. (I could use a few more—how about you?) The question to ask yourself is, how are you spending them? Is your life balanced or lopsided? Are you a workaholic? Are you taking care of your health? Your needs? It takes strength and perseverance to manage time well, smoothly and efficiently and still have time left to do all that we want to do.

Making time for yourself seems selfish, it seems unrealistic, and a lot of the time it's almost impossible. Fill in the blank: I'd love to _____, but I just don't have the time. What usually goes in that blank? I'm not talking about cleaning the garage; I'm talking about something that will make your spirit happy. Something that, if you do it, will give you a smile and a sense of pride. (Okay, you can clean the garage if you really want to.) It could be something you used to love but have stopped doing. It could be something that you've always wanted to try. How long has this idea been running around in your mind? Whatever it is, it's your heart yearning to do something that you seem to have been ignoring.

Imagine that a Wicked Witch visited you and turned over your hourglass, and you only had a week to live. What would you do in that week? I bet there are a few things that you might regret you haven't done, and a week wouldn't be enough time to complete them. (Luckily for you and me, this is just an exercise, and we've probably got more than a week left.) Put them on your list of things to do ASAP.

How about an hourglass with one year left? How about two years? How about five? It's quite a motivating exercise. It's an opportunity to see what really matters to you, and perhaps it might allow you to shift your priorities. Maybe a few of those items that were once on the "someday" list can actually get a date assigned to them, whether it is as far away as next November or as close as next Tuesday.

Dorothy experienced firsthand what she thought might be her final hour. You don't want to wait until that hour comes to realize that you needed more time. It's so easy to let time slip away. The years pass before you know it. Don't worry, there's still time for you to do all that you want to, see all the people and places you want to see. Be thankful for all the time you've had already, and plan your time so that later (much, much later—knock on wood) you won't have to would've, could've, should've. Be aware that every moment is a gift from the heavens, and use your time wisely.

The Winkies Whuppin'

Dorothy watches gravity funnel her minutes away in the hourglass. Toto runs to find her three pals and lead them to the Witch's castle. They are on the cliffs watching hundreds of the Witch's guards, the Winkies, march around. ("Oh-wee-oh. Woe-oh.") As they look upon the fortress, our fellas seem a bit intimidated. The Lion, of course, wants to forget the whole thing, but the Scarecrow has come up with a plan. As they huddle, plotting to rescue Dorothy, three Winkies ambush them. A brawl ensues, but they emerge triumphantly, dressed in the guards' outfits.

THE LESSON

I don't think anyone is more surprised than our threesome by the outcome of the fight. The Scarecrow, the Tin Man and the Cowardly Lion have been walking around telling themselves, "I've got no brain," "I've got no heart," "I'm a coward," and they have believed it for a very long time. Just like the trio, we sell ourselves short.

Who else but us can pull out a long list of our own faults? We know our weaknesses. We doubt ourselves, our strength and our power all the time. We are constantly putting ourselves down. I'm too fat. I'm not smart. I'm not good enough. Blah, blah, blah. My inner self-critic could go on for about three pages here, but let's just send her back to the dark recesses of my mind and move on.

Each self-deprecating thought takes away our power, and soon, just like these three, we start believing we are not smart enough, not loving enough and afraid of our own shadow. It's no wonder we are afraid to try to overcome things.

Life is like school on a larger scale, except now we are learning about ourselves—our strengths, our weaknesses, our faults and our fears. We are no longer getting grades but just trying to get through to the other side of a conflict, with as little drama as possible. In school there were times I was absolutely not prepared for a test, and most of the time I fared better than I expected. It's the same with struggles in life.

The truths we tell ourselves about ourselves always seem to underestimate our true abilities. The Lion would never have gotten into a fight with anyone, but when he was forced to, he found out he was filled with strength and courage, and he kicked some serious Winkie behind.

In our lives, it sometimes seems as if the world is testing our strength. We can go through difficult or trying times. Life can ambush us from behind and turn our lives into turmoil. Life does that to expand our vision of ourselves. We are strong. We are much more wise, loving, courageous and powerful than we can imagine. We can deal with, and emerge triumphant from, any situation.

No one likes a crisis, but when you have one, just remember the Lion and his pals. When you are put to the test, your strengths will surprise you.

Good Versus Evil

 **THE STORY**

The Scarecrow, the Tin Man and the Lion, disguised as Winkies (the Wicked Witch's guards), sneak into the castle. Toto leads them to where the Witch has imprisoned Dorothy. The Tin Man chops down the door (finally using that ax he's been lugging around for the entire movie). They make a run for it, but the Witch sees them. A castle chase ensues. Eventually they are trapped in a tower atop the castle—surrounded. The Witch is now ready to do away with them one by one.

Witch
The last to go will see the
first three go before her!
And her mangy little dog, too!

She sets her broomstick on fire with one of the castle torches.

> **Witch**
> How about a little fire, Scarecrow?

She lowers the broomstick, slowly igniting the Scarecrow's elbow. Dorothy, panicked, grabs a nearby bucket of water and throws it on him, putting out the flame. Some of the water hits the Wicked Witch in the face, and as she starts to melt, her voice fades away.

> **Witch**
> Oh—you cursed brat! Look what you've done!
> I'm melting! Melting! Oh—what a world—what a world.
> Who would've thought a good little girl like you
> could destroy my beautiful wickedness!? Oh!

All that is left of her is her pile of smoldering black clothes. (And the reason behind her sickly green hue is illuminated: 'Twas the years of not showering.)

THE LESSON

The *Wizard of Oz* has at its ending the same moral that has been repeated in perhaps half the movies ever made. There's a good guy. (A sheriff, a policeman, a suave spy who drinks martinis or a hipster swinger from the seventies with really bad teeth.) There's a bad guy. (An outlaw, a criminal, a supersize guy with gold teeth or a pale, bald madman with an effeminate pinky finger who wants to destroy the world.) In the end, the good guy always gets the bad guy, and we, the audience, are thrilled. It's a moral that we can get behind: Good triumphs over evil.

Our story appears to follow the very same theme. We've got a nice Kansas gal in gingham and a Wicked Witch, sporting the ever-popular black garb, who wants to kill her. And in the end the good gal ends up destroying the evil one.

Upon further contemplation of this scene, I have come to realize that the Oz story is a step ahead of most movies. It's true that in the end the Witch gets what's coming to her, and Dorothy's actions are what lead to her demise, but Dorothy's intentions are unlike those of most movie heroes. Most movie good guys go through the movie trying to catch the bad guy or wanting to destroy him. Dorothy was never out to get the Witch; it just happened as a result of trying to stop a friend from being burned alive.

The famous moral would be modified slightly for the Oz story to read: Good intentions will always triumph. Dorothy was not taking the law into her own hands; she wasn't trying to kill anybody or stop anyone or hurt them because they were bad and deserved it. All she wanted to do was go home. The Witch and her evil were a separate entity independent of Dorothy. Their story lines intertwined because Dorothy happened to have those pretty red shoes, and she needed to get the Witch's broomstick. But Dorothy never wavered from her original purpose of trying to find her way back to Kansas.

Although she was a tad concerned about the Witch's threats, Dorothy didn't let the old bag influence what she was doing. She minded her own business and tried to get home. Even though the Witch was after her, she managed to make some friends, skip a little and have some fun along the way.

Dorothy is the goddess of good intentions. Goodness comes from that place inside you that you know to be true, honest and acting with integrity in everything you do. And that is how Dorothy is. She never meant to hurt anybody. (Granted, she somehow turned into a serial witch killer, but that's just a fluke.) She was trying to save her friend—which is noble and true. She was acting with a good heart.

Whatever the issue in your life, if you choose to act with honest motivations, from a place of goodness, you can be confident that your choices will create valuable experiences and help you conquer the problem. It's how it works. Call it karma, call it divine law, call it whatever you want, but the energy that is behind good is ten times more powerful than anything negative or evil. (Okay, I have not scientifically proven this, but someday someone will—I'm sure of it.)

This is such a great lesson from Dorothy's journey and one of the big challenges in life. We need to stay focused on our purpose with a pure mind and spirit. Like Dorothy, we should not let the negativity of others who are trying to thwart us stop our progression through life. We need to believe that the wicked witches will eventually end up melting away if we continue to follow our paths of truth and integrity. In the end, we will be the heroines of our lives, and our good intentions will always triumph.

Back to See the Wizard

 **THE STORY**

Dorothy, the Scarecrow, the Tin Man and the Cowardly Lion return triumphantly, with the Wicked Witch's broomstick, to see the Wizard. They are excited to get some brains, a heart, courage and a way home to Kansas.

Dorothy
We've brought you the broomstick of the
Wicked Witch of the West. We melted her.

Oz's Voice
Oh, you liquidated her, eh? Very resourceful!

Dorothy
Yes, sir. So we'd like you to keep your promise to us,
if you please, sir.

Oz's Voice

Not so fast! Not so fast! I'll have to give the matter
a little thought. Go away and come back tomorrow!

Dorothy

Tomorrow? Oh, but I want to go home now. . . .
If you were really great and powerful,
you'd keep your promises!

THE LESSON

"A promise is a promise"—we hear that phrase all the time, but what does
it mean?

In this case, the Wizard has made quite a few big promises, and now
he is having second thoughts. Dorothy and gang have fulfilled their end
of the agreement and are asking the Wizard to do the same. The Wizard
is being a weasel, trying to go back on his promise. It seems almost cruel
of the Wizard to hem and haw over this after they've already risked life
and limb to get the broomstick. Dorothy is determined not to let the Wizard off the hook. She demands that he do what he said he'd do.

If asked, "Should people keep their promises?" everyone would answer, "Yes, of course, what a silly question." But do people always keep
their promises? No, not all the time.

A classic example is politicians. When campaigning, they make a ton
of promises, and then when they get into office, very often they don't
keep them. Because there are so many offenders, it's a pretty common
belief that all politicians are untrustworthy.

We expect politicians to break their promises, but when people in our lives do it, we feel cheated and disappointed. We can get hurt or mad or feel betrayed. We have a right to all of our feelings. Like Dorothy, we need to speak up and let others know when they are letting us down and not being honorable.

Most of us don't think of ourselves as promise breakers. We fully intend to stick to the things we say we'll do. Sometimes it's just the really big promises that are hard to keep because we've promised to do more than we think we are able to. Sometimes the little promises don't seem that important. Or perhaps it's when the conversation starts with, "You can't tell anyone else about this," and then a juicy piece of gossip is relayed. (The second anyone says this, the secret becomes even harder to keep—why is that?)

A promise is a statement of our true self, our integrity and our reputation. One consequence of an unkept promise is that it is hurtful to the people the promise was made to. But the other consequence is that we are traveling down that slippery slope that may lead to our proving we are not trustworthy, that we are not to be believed. (If we're not careful, soon we'll start campaigning and kissing babies.) Not keeping our word not only shatters others' belief in us but pokes a tiny hole in their trust in all people. We are contributing to the belief that "you can't trust anyone."

It is probably impossible to keep every single promise, but we can at least examine how we make and break promises in our lives and try our best to keep them. When do you have a hard time keeping your word? Are you always saying you'll do things and then forgetting about them? Are you overcommitting yourself and then having to back out? You might even want to ask your closest friends and your family members to give you a grade on how well they feel you follow through on your promises.

The hardest promises to keep are the ones we make to ourselves. How about those New Year's resolutions? They get us every time. The only one I've managed to keep is the one I made about five years ago: I resolved not to make any more New Year's resolutions.

I mean to keep my promises to myself, but somehow I don't. I'm going to finish this project by a certain date, clean out the closet and the ever-popular, "Next week, I promise, I'm starting that diet!" It never fails. My personal deadlines come and go, and what are the consequences? I get mad at myself, feel bad about not sticking to that weight-loss program and end up eating an entire bag of Doritos.

The harder it is to keep a promise, the harder we should try. The challenge is to our moral fiber. If we can't do what we say, how are we ever going to begin to teach our children to do the same? How can we expect others to do the same for us? How can we ask politicians to keep their promises?

Like Dorothy, demand that people in your life keep their promises to you—especially if you have held up your end of the bargain. If you make no other promises to yourself, promise to try your best to keep your promises.

Behind the Curtain

 THE STORY

Dorothy and friends are still standing before the levitating Wizard's surly countenance waiting for their requests to be granted, when Toto (still unleashed) sees something off in the corner. Toto mysteriously pulls back a green curtain to reveal the not-so-wonderful, not-so-great-and-powerful wizard, who is just a man at a control panel talking into a microphone and operating the Wizard of Oz special effects.

The man closes the curtain.

Oz's voice (bellowing)
Pay no attention to that man behind the curtain.
The great Oz has spoken!

Dorothy walks over and opens the drapery and addresses the man.

Dorothy
Who are you?

Oz's voice (meekly)
Well, uh, I am the great and powerful Wizard of Oz.

THE LESSON

The Wizard of Oz seems great and powerful. He seems very intimidating. Who wouldn't be afraid of a levitating green head that with every shout is accompanied by booming thunder?

No matter how much money a person has—whether it's a gazillionaire or a street person; no matter the position—the president of the United States or your boss; no matter what the person's temperament—an air of authority or a general grumpiness; no one is any better than you are.

The people we look up to in the world—the leaders, the sports figures and the heads of corporations, people who appear to have power (and sometimes big bank accounts)—are no different from the Wizard. In reality they are just people.

The fame, the fortune, are just illusions. The things we have been told about them are a bunch of smoke and mirrors. They are made from the same stuff as you and me. They were born, they were raised, and they played in the sprinkler in the summertime. They may have had more money, but what about the things money can't buy? They may have been awkward, pimply teenagers who were nervous and unsure of themselves. I love to hear the stories of the tall, gangly models who didn't have dates for the prom and of the millionaires who flunked out of college.

We don't always hear about these people in their everyday lives. We get only the big, important, exciting news, spun by their spokespersons and usually dealing with their public lives. Not the private ones, where they roll out of bed and feel like crap and want to hit the snooze button on their alarm clock for the rest of the day. The president has to get up and brush his teeth in the morning (among other things), just like you and me. What's the difference? (We were smart and stayed out of politics!)

The great and powerful are only great and powerful because we have given them the power. They are just people with the same problems we have. They still have challenges in their lives, heartache, disappointments, health problems and bad days. They face the same issues we face on a daily basis. Am I making the right decision? Am I dong the right thing? Am I being a good parent?

We are all human, experiencing life, trying to get by and do the best we can. We all have feelings, and we all get them hurt sometimes. We all have hearts that want to love. We are all the sum of our experiences, and that is what makes us uniquely us. Just because the Wizard has obtained the title of Wizard doesn't make him any more special than we are. A pedestal is not where anybody should be placed, because from there they can only fall.

Like everyone, great leaders have their weaknesses. They might be great at politics but bad at love. A CEO might be good at running a company but have a home life that is a disaster. We all have our faults, and we all are trying to live our lives to the best of our abilities.

It's easy to be intimidated by people, especially by people in our immediate sphere who seem more important and more powerful than we are. Our bosses can sometimes intimidate us. And unarguably, they do have an influence over our work lives, but sometimes, working under people, we give too much of our power away. We kowtow to unreasonable demands and, out of fear, agree to do whatever is asked of us.

Friends and family members can sometimes bully us. It's because we have given them power over us. Some people like to try to make us feel less than they are because it makes them feel important.

Are there people in your life who intimidate you? Whom you shy away from? Is there anyone in your life whom you allow to bully you? Are there people you have given power over you?

Why do we give them preferred status? Why do we think they are more important? Why do we get intimidated instead of speaking our minds? We have built them up to be more than they are. They are not as powerful as we think.

We give away our power because in some parts of ourselves, we don't feel we are good enough or smart enough or have the ability to change our lives. The power we give to them is really just an indication of our feelings of inadequacy. If we felt confident about our position in regard to them, we would not feel intimidated.

When we give other people Wizard of Oz status, it's useful to remember what happened in the movie. When Toto pulled back the curtain, they found a humble, caring, nice man. He admitted that he was very bad at being a wizard, but he tried to be a good person.

Remember that wizards in your life are no better, and no more important, than you are. If you treat people as equals, they will treat you as an equal. If you give them preferred status, that is your doing and not theirs. Certain people may seem great and powerful, but really, like the Wizard, they are just like you and me.

Promises Kept

 **THE STORY**

The Wizard of Oz is discovered to be just a man, and the foursome is quite disappointed. They came all that way to get some brains, a heart and some courage, and now what are they to do? The Wizard has humbly expressed his regret for being a poor wizard but has explained that they each already possess the quality that they long for.

The Wizard presents the Scarecrow with an honorary degree as proof that he in fact has a brain. The Wizard pins a medal on the Cowardly Lion to reward him for his bravery, and it will remind him that he has courage. Bestowed upon the Tin Man is a heart-shaped clock, ticking away so that he'll never forget that he has a heart.

THE LESSON

Dorothy's three pals have traveled a very long way, climbed mountains, fought flying monkeys and faced the wickedest witch of all to get the things that they felt would make them complete. The Wizard enlightens them with this little tidbit of information: You have what you've been looking for all along.

If we go back and look through the story, it is quite evident that for each one this is true. The Scarecrow thought he needed a brain, but from the moment we met him, he had one. In the very first scene, when the Scarecrow is still stuck up on a pole and Dorothy is attempting to help him down, he tells her:

> Of course, I'm not bright about doing things,
> but if you'll just bend the nail down in the back,
> maybe I'll slip off.

The Scarecrow slides easily off the pole.

Later on in the story, the Scarecrow comes up with the plan to get into the Witch's castle. His brain has been working the entire time—he just doesn't realize it.

Throughout the story, the Tin Man is very emotional, proving that he has a heart. When Dorothy falls asleep in the poppy field, the Tin Man starts bawling. He also gets a little weepy when they first see the Wicked Witch's castle because he can't bear to think of Dorothy in such an evil place. He manages to save Dorothy because he loves her. For someone who claims not to have a heart, the Tin Man does quite a lot of crying and caring.

And last but not least, the Cowardly Lion has tons of courage. He fights the Witch's guards and goes in to rescue Dorothy. If that's not courage, I don't know what is.

The same is true in our lives: The qualities that we think we are lacking are there waiting to be expressed. We have to be willing to take a journey, travel through some scary forests and battle some wicked witches. We have to be prepared to confront them in order to move past that limited vision of ourselves.

The qualities that we most would like to have are already within us. They are hidden jewels waiting to shine as brilliantly as the Lion's medal, to dazzle everyone around us. What is that quality in your life? Can you think of specific instances when that aspect of yourself was prominent (just as we listed them for our heroes)? Whatever the attribute—to be understanding, to be outgoing, to be content, to be filled with joy—you can bring it to the surface.

Our lives are like one of those optical illusion 3-D pictures. At first glance we are only able to see one flat image. If we look at it long enough, our line of vision expands, and the 3-D picture pops out at us.

We need to look at our lives differently, to adjust our vision in order to see a more complete, three-dimensional image of ourselves. The image will be more apparent the more experiences we have that contradict our limiting beliefs and negative self-images. We've got to dispel these thoughts of "I'm not loving," "I'm not courageous" and "I'm not [fill in the blank]."

Like an archaeologist, we must be prepared to wander around in search of our true nature. When we find a tiny example that it exists, it's as if we have uncovered our very first glimpse of what lies underneath our surface. We must be willing to work slowly, painstakingly, one tiny piece at a time, to uncover that beautiful relic. We can use all of our tools—our friends, family or experts—to gain new wisdom and insight about our lives and ourselves. The more we dust and try to uncover, the more of our true nature will be revealed.

In this moment, right now, you have what you've been looking for all along.

There's No Place Like Home

THE END OF THE STORY

After the Wizard presents our heroes with awards for wisdom, love and courage, he has nothing to fulfill Dorothy's wish to go home. He decides to take Dorothy back to Kansas in his hot-air balloon. All of Emerald City is there for the spectacular send-off. As the Wizard and Dorothy are about to leave, Toto leaps out of Dorothy's arms and chases a cat. (Isn't that what got them into this predicament in the first place?)

Dorothy jumps out of the balloon and runs after him. The Wizard doesn't really know how to fly the contraption, and off it ascends without her, leaving Dorothy still stuck in Oz. Glinda, in her gigantic Bazooka bubble, floats down through the crowd to come to Dorothy's rescue.

Dorothy
Oh, will you help me? Can you help me?

Glinda

You don't need to be helped any longer.

You've always had the power to go back to Kansas.

Dorothy

I have?

Scarecrow

Then why didn't you tell her before?

Glinda

Because she wouldn't have believed me.

She had to learn it for herself.

Tin Man

What have you learned, Dorothy?

Dorothy

Well, I think that it—that it wasn't enough just to

want to see Uncle Henry and Auntie Em—

and it's that—if I ever go looking for

my heart's desire again, I won't look any further

than my own backyard. Because if it isn't there,

I never really lost it to begin with! Is that right?

Glinda

That's all it is!

Dorothy says her goodbyes and clicks those magic ruby heels three times.

> **Dorothy**
>
> There's no place like home.
> There's no place like home.
> There's no place like home.

Dorothy is magically transported to her room, back in Kansas, where she awakens, lying in her bed, to find Uncle Henry, the farmhands and Auntie Em by her side. She tells them all about her trip, and they tell her it was all just a dream.

> **Dorothy**
> No, Aunt Em—this was a real, truly live place.
> And I remember that some of it wasn't
> very nice but most of it was beautiful.
> But just the same,
> all I kept saying to everybody was,
> I want to go home.
> And they sent me home. . . .
> And this is my room—and you're all here!
> And I'm not going to leave here ever,
> ever again, because I love you all!
> And—oh Auntie Em—
> there's no place like home!

THE BIG LESSONS

At the end of a long journey, one would hope for pearls of wisdom that might leave us a little more enlightened, a bit more inspired and quite a bit happier than when we first started down the path with Dorothy. This last scene is the culmination of Dorothy's trip, and for me, four major lessons stand out (aside from the obvious "Buy your dog a damn leash!" lesson).

- ❧ What are you learning?

- ❧ Wherever you go, wisdom, love and courage will help get you there.

- ❧ You've always had the power . . .

- ❧ Your heart's desire is no further than your own backyard. (There's no place like home.)

What Are You Learning?

When Glinda tells Dorothy she always had the power to go back to Kansas, most of us react as the Scarecrow does. I know I would have used more than a few expletives: "Why the #*&$@! didn't you tell her that before?" Glinda's response is that Dorothy had to learn it for herself.

I can only assume that, since you are at the end of a book titled *Lessons from Oz*, you are one of those people who attempt to figure out this thing called life. You understand that the ability to learn is one of the greatest gifts of being human. I have always thought that if we knew all we needed to know, then we probably wouldn't be here. We would have been something much easier—like a cat (ah, yes, sleeping and eating all the livelong day), or perhaps a flower (looking good is the only requirement) or maybe a rock (just sitting there). As people, we have been given this amazing life filled with boundless opportunities for learning.

From the second we were born, we started to learn. First we had to figure out how to communicate with our parents, who then started to teach us about life. We went to school and spent at least 12 years obtaining knowledge. When we graduated, the teaching did not stop. It just took on a new form in our adult lives. Our learning became not just about facts and figures but about answers to the bigger questions: What is true happiness? What is true love? What is my life about? What am I supposed to be doing?

Our lives are a unique series of events to help us answer those questions. Life is definitely here to teach us something, and for each of us the lesson plan is different. No amount of information our parents told us, or our teachers taught us, can get us through the life lessons we are to be taught. Unfortunately, just as Glinda said, we have to learn it for ourselves.

And it's best to learn lessons the first time around. Life has this funny way of repeating experiences until we appreciate and understand fully what we are supposed to know. If the same situations keep happening over and over, that's life whispering in our ear: "Pssst, there's something you might want to catch on to here."

If we are constantly learning about ourselves and how we react to situations, our lives will become better and better. We will make wiser decisions, allowing us to have more enjoyable lives instead of dealing with one hardship after another. We know that in this story Dorothy will think twice about running away from home again. She'll remember her stint over the rainbow and know that her heart's desire is no further than her own backyard. She can avoid another excursion to an Oz-like place altogether.

Dorothy's interlude in Oz ends with a major lesson, but our lives are a series of adventures filled with endless epiphanies. Our goal is to keep learning, for if we don't, then we are no better than a rock. Each day can bring new insight and understanding.

You can find lessons everywhere. Obviously, I like to reflect upon life based on my favorite movie, *The Wizard of Oz*. Each time you ask yourself, "What have I learned?" you can feel proud to be in the company of Dorothy. Whatever the lesson, no matter if it's heart-wrenching or wonderful, embrace it and know that you are a little bit farther along on your path. You can smile and think that, yes, it would have been so much easier knowing all this a long time ago, but the learning is in the journey. With each lesson comes wisdom, and the ability to lead a life more fully realized.

Wherever You Go, Wisdom, Love and Courage Will Help Get You There

Wherever you go, whatever you are searching for, no matter what obstacle you are trying to overcome, you won't get very far without the big three—wisdom, love and courage. On her journey, Dorothy traveled with three friends who personified these qualities.

The Tin Man, the Scarecrow and the Cowardly Lion were there to help her. They pointed her down the right path along the Yellow Brick Road. They were beside her through the dark and creepy forest. They rescued her from the Wicked Witch's castle. Even though Dorothy was over the rainbow, far from home and lost, her adventure through Oz, while filled with setbacks, was one of joy, and lots of singing and dancing, because of the company she was keeping.

Wisdom, love and courage reside inside us all. The degree to which we develop these qualities and let them radiate through our lives will help determine whether we have a happier and easier journey.

Each character has his own chapter, but here's a quick review:

Like the Scarecrow, we need to use our brains to think great thoughts and to help see the crux of any issue. All we need to do is take the time to get centered and consult our inner wisdom to thoughtfully answer any question concerning our lives, and to ultimately illuminate our perfect path.

Like the Tin Man, we have a need to love and be loved. Our capacity to love is limitless. If we can approach all aspects of our lives from a place of love, instead of reacting from a place of anger or sadness, we will create more and more positive experiences, and those negative emotions will be greatly reduced. Whenever we call upon this pure emotion, it has the ability to transform our lives.

Like the Lion, we sometimes let our fear run our lives. Fear is a paralyzing emotion—one that will keep us stuck in the same place, too afraid to live our lives to their fullest potential. We must have courage. Courage is not the absence of fear but the ability to confront a fear head-on and deal with it. If we stand up to our fears, we can overcome doubts and sinking-stomach feelings. If we dare to find the courage within us, we will, like the Lion, emerge victorious, happy, and filled with pride that those fears are no longer holding us back from being what we were meant to be.

Wherever your path takes you in life, remember, you have wisdom, love and courage in your arsenal. All you need to do is wisely think it through, confront the situation with love in your heart and have the courage to stand up to your fears, and, like Dorothy, you will be skipping most of the way.

You've Always Had The Power . . . *

Glinda told Dorothy that she'd always had the power to go back to Kansas. With luck, it won't take you a long journey, a complete breakdown or an angry witch on your tail to realize it, but the power Glinda was talking about is also within you right now.

If you knew you had the power to do anything you wanted with your life, what would you do? Where does your spirit beckon you? In the direction of a new career? Making a difference in the world? Less stress and more joy? Fulfilling relationships? Happiness instead of sadness?

The power within you is there anytime you need it, and it is happy to help you accomplish all that and more. All you have to do is realize you have it and tap into it—which is sometimes easier said than done.

On a lot of days, I have to admit, I don't feel that powerful. Heck, sometimes I barely have enough verve to get out of bed in the morning, let alone completely reinvent my world. Most of the time I'm just trying to get through my day without incident, have a little fun, do my job and not stress out. My life is pretty humdrum, and it doesn't occur to me all that often to think about my power.

---

*As much as I would like to take full credit for this lesson, I cannot. In the middle of writing this book, I was lucky enough to hear one of the most thoughtful and amazing talks given by Oprah Winfrey in her "Live Your Best Life" seminar in Los Angeles. She has been a heroine of mine for quite some time, and I find her show inspirational beyond words. She is my own personal TV Glinda, keeping me on my path, speaking truth and wisdom and many lessons I have needed to hear. So, during her seminar, my jaw just about dropped to the floor when she started talking about her favorite life lesson from the movie *The Wizard of Oz*. While I didn't take notes, and I wrote this chapter much later, I still think of this as Oprah's lesson. Thanks, Oprah!

That, I guess, is my problem (and was also Dorothy's). Usually I am not acknowledging this power within, which means I am disconnected from it. As with any kind of energy, you need to turn on the switch to be able to use it.

What is this power, exactly?

This power is your life energy, your spirit, the core of who you are. It's hard to describe where this essence of you is, but you could say it's where your brain and your heart meet. It is that very center of your being where you know the truth of who you are—that recognizes that no matter your troubles, your day-to-day self-doubts and setbacks, when all is said and done, you are wonderful. You are here in this world, living right now, for a reason, and there will never be anyone else quite like you. Focusing on your true self is how you can cultivate your inner power to lead an amazing life. It can be the force behind all that you do.

To find that center, you need to be still. You can shut your eyes and focus. (Clicking your heels is optional.) It can be found by meditating or just by sitting quietly. Experiencing that stillness is similar to consulting your inner wisdom, but it goes a bit deeper. Instead of asking yourself a question, you're trying to get to the core of your being. You'll need to let go of all stress, all worries, and release all bad, unproductive thoughts until there is just this lovely, centered self.

In that space, you need to appreciate yourself—all those great qualities that are strung together to make you. What are they? Make a list. See if you can get to one hundred words to sing your praises. Loving. Caring. Honest. Smart. Insightful. What are the things that you are proud of about yourself? And your life? Try to fill a page with your empowering truths. I am courageous. I laugh whenever possible. I am a loving person. I try to do my best at all times. I have raised a terrific kid. I am grateful. I am silly. Making a point of acknowledging all that you are is like filling your tank with gas.

Try adding the phrase "I am powerful" to your list of truths. At first it may seem a bit conceited or grandiose. But this is your mission, and if you choose to accept it, it will change your life, and there is no turning back.

Once we claim that we *are* all that and a bag of chips, we cannot be less than that anymore. We can't go around whining and complaining about our lives or other people—being victims, blaming others or concentrating on our faults and our weaknesses. We know that we can and will overcome these obstacles. Once we start believing we are powerful, sitting around and watching TV every waking minute is just not an option. We want to lead extraordinary lives, right? Of course! But be forewarned, extraordinary lives take determination and hard work. Great, rewarding, life-altering work! As you learn to tap into and focus on your own personal energy, you can begin to make your life happen the way you'd like it to.

You were not brought to this earth to be sad or lonely, or angry, or not good enough, or depressed, or a victim. None of those are on your list of truths.

You are meant to be happy. You are meant to be fulfilled. You are meant to be loving and joyous and generous and grateful and to shine the truth of who you are wherever you go. That truth is your power. That truth will motivate you. That truth will keep you on track, keep you working toward challenging yourself to live your life to its highest potential.

We have the power to manifest whatever we want for ourselves, and that is a huge responsibility. We have the ability to create a fulfilling life surrounded by love, joy and wonder, and friends and family.

No matter where you have landed in this life, you can find your way back. What are you waiting for? Remember Glinda's words, "You've always had the power." So close your eyes, start clicking those heels, and let them take you where you want to go.

There's No Place Like Home

At the beginning of the story, Dorothy wished she were somewhere over the rainbow instead of on that dreary old farm. She was disenchanted with her life and thought things might be better somewhere else.

We spend a lot of time wishing for our perfect world, just like Dorothy's vision of what "over the rainbow" would be like. "I wish I lived somewhere else." "I wish I had a different job." "I wish I had more money." "If only my life were completely different, then I'd be happy!" We live under the misguided notion that the circumstances that surround our lives are the reasons behind our discontent.

When Dorothy gets her wish and lands in that magical place over the rainbow, she realizes that as fantastic and wonderful as it is, it's not perfect there either. Oz has its problems—there are flying monkeys and wicked witches and a city that is entirely green.

After her jaunt through Oz, she decides that home is not such a bad place to be. In fact, that is her big lesson in the end. "If I ever go looking for my heart's desire again, I won't look any further than my own backyard."

Our own backyards are the furthest we need to go to find our hearts' desire—some might call it happiness.

To find true happiness, you don't need to travel over the rainbow, to Paris or some other faraway place. You don't have to have your dream job, a gazillion dollars or some fairy-tale romance. Happiness is attainable in your life, right now—even if you have problems up the wazoo, even with the bills piling up, even with the stress and aggravation of everyday life. The secret to true happiness is to love your life in spite of all those things you might want to change about it, all those things that don't seem to be going right, all the setbacks and worries that are continually thrown in your direction.

You will constantly be faced with one challenge after another in your life. Your attitude and emotional responses to these challenges can either keep you in a state of distress or help you to work through any situation with ease. Dorothy, even though far from home, was able to skip through the movie, sing and dance and have a great time. She didn't spend the entire movie moaning about what a drag it was to be stuck in Oz.

The one moment she did break down was when she realized that she didn't appreciate her life back home. Being away from home was an opportunity to realize all the things that were good in her life back on the farm.

We need to appreciate all the blessings in our lives. It's easy to get caught up in complaints about what is not going right. Keeping a more positive outlook and a grateful heart can lead us to contentment. Dorothy's farm life was exactly the same before she went to Oz and after she came back. It was only her view of it that changed. She realized how much she had on the farm—a life filled with family and friends who loved her and who were always there for her.

Your own happiness is actually much closer than your backyard—your happiness lies within you. If you are not fulfilled and happy, then only you can fix that. You must look at your life to see what work you need to do—where you might need to open up and think new thoughts and start to change your life so that it is one filled with love, joy and laughter despite the hardships.

As you skip down your Yellow Brick Road of life, ignore those pesky wicked witches that may try to thwart your progress. Travel with wisdom, love and courage. Remember, whatever you are searching for, you already have it—you just need to learn that yourself. The power to create your most wonderful life lies within you at all times. Don't look outside yourself to find your heart's desire—it is always right where you are. The dreams that you dare to dream really will come true, because you will make them happen, and just like Dorothy, you will find your way home to your own true bliss.

Permissions

Notes

Hey, you took my advice and even checked my facts! Crime statistics are updated all the time, and these were the most recent published facts (that were from a legitimate source) that I could find before the book was printed.

Lions and Tigers and Bears! Oh, My!

1 **Average life expectancy in the U.S. is 77.9 years.**
"Deaths: Preliminary Data for 2004," *National Center For Health Statistics, Health E-Stats*, Table 1, January 11, 2007.
http://www.cdc.gov/nchs/data/hestat/preliminarydeaths04tables.pdf#1

2 **The average murder rate, according to the United States Crime Index, per 100,000 inhabitants, was 5.6 in 1966 and 5.6 in 2005.**
"US Crime Rates 1960–2005," *The Disaster Center*, February 4, 2007.
http://www.disastercenter.com/crime/uscrime.htm

3 **The average violent-crime rate, according to the United States Crime Index, per 100,000 inhabitants, was 487.8 in 1975 and 469.2 in 2005.**
"US Crime Rates 1960–2005," *The Disaster Center*, February 4, 2007.
http://www.disastercenter.com/crime/uscrime.htm

Acknowledgments

Thanks ever so to everybody who bought this book. I am eternally grateful that you spent your hard-earned cash. I hope you liked it. Thank you! Thank you! Thank you!

First off, there are a few main people I need to thank for getting this thing out of my computer and into the world.

To the copy-editing maven, **Linda Goldstein**, who made my writing readable: Thank you for your constant support, commitment, diligence and patience. I appreciate the gentle elegance of your notes ("I think it might be better this way...."). Your graceful honesty helped me get rid of those unneeded chapters. Without you, this book would be just a bunch of personal ramblings with tons of poor grammar! I know you didn't plan on getting yourself into this, but I am so grateful that you were not only the best editor ever but a really great friend too.

To the queen of design, **Mauna Eichner** (and her partner, **Lee Fukui**), thank-yous until the end of time for your awe-inspiring design. Who cares what all these words say? It's a work of art! It's spectacular! Thank you for motivating me to get this done when you hadn't heard from me in a while, for putting up with all my crazy suggestions (how about a rainbow?) and for treating this book as if it were your very own.

I need to thank everyone at Warner Bros. in a number of different departments who gave the okay to use parts of their classic movie. Without them, the book in my mind's eye would never have been possible. For those fabulous photos, **Marlene Eastman**, **Darlene Grodske** and **Geoff Murrillo**. (Searching the archives was one of my favorite parts of putting this book together.) For the quotes, a big thanks to **Judy Noack** and **Shannon Fifer**. For the lyrics, **David Olsen**.

Thanks so very much to **Kathy Brown** for your commitment, patience, and suggestions that made this book lovely, and to my fellow Michiganders at Sheridan Books for all your hard work. It looks amazing!

To **Ryan Lapidus** (and his team of very smart fellas), a ton of thanks for your great counsel and completely honest advice. Thanks for always checking in and being so supportive.

And to **Kevin Cleary:** In the long line of "Thanks, but no thanks," you were the first one to say, "I love this!" Thanks for negotiating the quotes and trying your damnedest to peddle *Lessons from Oz*. If I typed out a "thank you" for every late-night walk and talk spent convincing my inner neurotic writer that she knows what she is doing, I could never have afforded to print this. You are definitely the Pep Talk King. (It's good, right?)

I hope everyone in my life knows that I couldn't have done this without them. Since nobody but people who know the author reads the acknowledgments, I've made it easy—it's alphabetical.

Auntie Em: You are definitely the reason I identified with Dorothy from the start. That, and growing with up your uncanny ability to style my hair just like hers. P.S. You are a lot nicer than the movie version! **Janine & Dave Bauer:** (see Neener) **L. Frank Baum:** It didn't feel right not to thank the wizard of Oz himself, the creative genius, ahead of his time, who wrote this story. So wherever you are, thanks for such a heartwarming, life-changing, magical tale. **Barbara Blesma:** To the most beautiful Aunt Barb, godmother extraordinaire, thank you for all the inspiration throughout the years. (That's what you said, isn't it?) **Linda Brown:** Well, my BFF, I am pretty sure you have been with me since the beginning of my Oz fascination, and you have been there for me every step of my life. My only wish is that my ruby slippers were real so I could click my heels whenever I wanted to spend more time with you. The book tour awaits, and I hope you're ready. **Michelle Crehan:** Thank you for the most inspirational phrase—"Your dreams are the blueprints to your destiny"—and for all your sage advice along the way. **Emma Ford:** (see Auntie Em) **Gal on Jury Duty:** It's been so long since we went to lunch, I've forgotten your name, but I wanted to give you credit and say thanks for the spa-day lesson idea. **Chris Haston:** Thanks for taking the most beautiful picture of ruby slippers never to be seen on bookshelves everywhere! **Hike Club (Al, Dave, Gabby & Jonathan):** I thank the heavens that our paths crossed and that you guys are my friends. Be it kickball, a book or a silly country ditty, thanks for rallying behind every one of my dreams and for always making me laugh/snort. **Jennifer Howald:** We've been wishing on rainbows since college, and this here is my pot o' gold, and even though we're far apart, you're always close to my heart. When you asked me to be a godmother, it made me realize my true spiritual side, which is the force behind this book. P.S. Thanks for *Wicked* on Broadway! **Lisa Jean:** We have been down 25 years of yellow brick roads together and made our L.A. dreams come true. Thanks for your words of clarity and definitive positivism and for always being a wonderful friend. **Matt LaFleur:** To my biggest littlest bro, thanks for all the cool Oz stuff—the Xmas ornament is my absolute favorite! (Shh. Don't tell Janine.) **Michele LaFleur:** Thanks for being the coolest stepmom ever and for always inquiring about the book and chatting about it to all your friends. **Shane LaFleur:** Little bro, thanks for spending all your dough on Oz goods and for always checking on my progress. I know you believed I'd get it done. **Marc Luperini:** So what do you know, I finally took paradise out of the box. Thanks for the phrase that kept the treasure hunt going until I had the gumption to see what was inside. Your turn. **Kristen McGary:** Girlie, I can't really express my thanks to you. (It would take pages.) Muchas gracias for being an amazing friend and the very first example of someone who said, "To heck with the safe, boring life!" and followed her bliss. You are an inspiration. **Stefanie Medina** (and her better half, **April**): Goddess of all things monetary, a thousand thank-yous for everything—incorporating, filing and helping me with all that paperwork! **Monica Muehlhouse-Horn:** Miss Thang, you have been around since the very start of this thing. Thank you for your steadfast support! **Neener:** Thanks for believing in my book and, of course, for your generosity for giving me the endless supply of Oz baubles—the cow dressed as Dorothy is my absolute favorite! (Shh. Don't tell Matt.) **Bob Powers:** Dearest super man in my life, thank you for being my friend and confidant. Your never-ending supply of love, good wishes and compliments keeps me going. Without your joy, happiness and philosophical counsel, my life just wouldn't be the same. Thanks, too, for being my first sale. Big hug to you! **Scott Roeben:** You have been a part of this from the beginning. Thanks for the first edit, the Web site, sending me a slew of silly signs weekly and just about a gazillion other things. Thank you from the bottom of my heart (you'll always have a special roped-off section in there). **Kim Seeley:** Thanks for the fabulous writers' retreats, for your unconditional support and for being the kind of friend who will always tell you when your zipper's down. **Lisa Shactman-Grissom:** Girl, what can I say? You are better than the best friend! Thank-yous until infinity for listening and for caring way too much about everything. I hope you know that I appreciate you and our friendship all the time (including randomly). You are my partner in crime, in silliness and in dream chasing. A hug and kiss to ya. And a big shout-out to the family—hey, Girrrl! **Donna Shepard:** Well, that's good idea #124 finished—now it's back atcha. Thanks for your last-minute input and very good eyes. P.S. The FTP looks forward to publishing your first book. **Leslie Shulem:** Thanks for being so darn courageous and getting me out of the plane. Without you, the chapter on courage would've fallen short. **Alexandra Wescourt:** Thank you for all your input as my resident Oz expert and for the ultimate question/suggestion, "Is the first half of the book going to be in black and white?" Ding-dong, the book is done, and the next Sing-A-Long is on me.

The idea for this book came about in a spiritual manner, so I wanted to thank my primary spiritual teachers in their very own section.

Mom and **Dad:** I originally learned all these lessons from you. Thank you both for believing in me and my dreams and for getting behind every single one of them. Thank you for your words of wisdom, for your shoulders to cry on, for always being there no matter what and for working so hard to make sure your kids had all they ever wanted (would you guys retire already?). You are the best parents a girl could ask for. I love you both a million-trillion-billion-infinity times around the world!

Rev. Roger Aldi: Thanks from the bottom of my soul! For without you, kind sir, and your meditation class, this book never would've been. Thanks for showing me the power of a quiet mind and a still small voice (or, in this case, a very loud and annoying one).

Rev. Dr. Michael Beckwith: Thanks ever so for bringing me back to my center whenever I am out of sorts. I am constantly in awe of your ability to inspire soul transformation through your wisdom and keen wit. I am lucky and honored to hear you as you change the universal consciousness one sermon at a time. P.S. To Rickie Beyers Beckwith and anyone who has ever musically graced the Agape stage: Your music rocks my soul, and thank you for every note. www.agapelive.com

Rev. Marlene Morris: Thank you with all my spirit! For coaxing my inner spiritual (and more enlightened) self out and for speaking about the world and universe in a way that finally made sense to me, completely changed, challenged and reinvented my life and made me realize who I am and what I am meant to do in the world. And, of course, thank you for the Oz lesson here in this book. www.marlenemorrisministries.com

Stephan Poulter, Ph.D.: Dr. P.—what can I say? A thousand thank-yous for keeping me on track, listening, being so damn insightful, calling me on all my crap, keeping my fear of death in check, always knowing just what to say that snaps me back to the Truth, for your constant mellow certainty that I would figure this book thing out and for your incredible connection to spirit that never ceases to amaze me! www.onefatherfactor.com

Oprah Winfrey (to anyone reading this, I don't personally know Ms. Winfrey, nor have I met her): You are an inspiration to so many people, and I can't thank you enough for challenging me on a daily basis to get out and do more with my life. Your intuitive honesty and uncanny ability to speak your spirit is a channel for spectacular, powerful changes in the world! www.oprah.com

God/the universe: Thank you for sending me along my *Lessons from Oz* path. Thanks for showering me with all of those Oz signs to make me smile. For being there in the still of 3:00 A.M. or whenever I needed guidance. I am so completely thankful and honored and overwhelmed to have been entrusted with this book. I am eternally grateful for this most amazing life! (Words are not enough.)

About the Author

Photograph by Dave Long

Julienne La Fleur does not have a Ph.D. in anything. But she does have a soulful connection to *The Wizard of Oz*, and it always makes her spirit happy to watch it. She lives in Southern California with her dog, Miss Moxie Moo. *Lessons from Oz* is her first book.